The Works of Saint Patrick of Ireland

The Works of
Saint Patrick of Ireland

Translated from the original Latin

Translator: Michael Gray

Editor: Luann Zanzola

The Latin texts used in this volume were obtained from Jacques-Paul Migne's Patrologia Latina, *Volume 53*

Front Cover: The Virgin and Child, *The Book of Kells*
Back Cover: The Eight-Circled Cross, *The Book of Kells*

Cataloguing in-Publication Data
The Works of Saint Patrick of Ireland.
Gray, Michael—Translator.
Zanzola, Luann—Editor.

1. Saint Patrick. 2. Latin Translations. 3. Patron saint of Ireland
4. Irish legends. 5. Catholic Church history in Ireland.

Produced by Michael Gray. All rights reserved.
Published by Amazon's Kindle Direct Publishing (KDP).
ISBN-13: 979-861-5049590
First printed March 5, 2020.

Table of Contents

Part 1: Texts Written by Saint Patrick

Part 2: Texts Attributed to Saint Patrick

Part 3: Miscellaneous Texts

Part 1

Texts Written by Saint Patrick

The Confession
Written to the Irish as a Letter

I, Patrick, am a sinner, the simplest and least of all the faithful—and the most contemptible to many. My father was the Deacon Calpurnius, and his father was Potitius the Elder, now deceased, from the village of Bonavem Taberniae. Nearby, in the village of Enon, when I was roughly 16 years old, I was captured and, along with a thousand other men, was taken in captivity to Ireland. We deserved this because we had wandered from God and did not keep his precepts, and because we were not obedient to our priests, who reminded us of our salvation. The Lord brought the anger of his being upon us, scattering us in many countries, all the way to the end of the earth, where now my small self is seen among foreigners. Thus, the Lord revealed my unbelief to me, so that even at this late hour, I would remember my offenses and return with my whole heart to the Lord, my God. He looked upon my lowliness and had pity on my youth and ignorance. He guarded me before I knew him, before I could think sensibly or distinguish between good and evil. He protected and consoled me, as a father does his son.

Therefore, I cannot be silent. The Lord has shown me so much kindness and grace in the land of my captivity that I must repay him, despite my imprisonment, by praising the knowledge of God and openly confessing his wonders to every nation under heaven. God the Father lives; there never was, and never will be, another god besides him. He is unbegotten and without beginning, yet from him everything has its beginning, and he holds everything together in himself. We believe his son, Jesus Christ, was with the Father before time began. He is one in being with the Father and was born before all beginnings. Through him all things visible and invisible were made. He became man, conquered death, and the Father received him in heaven. The Father gave Jesus Christ all power, put his name above every other name in heaven, on earth, and under the earth, so every tongue will confess that Jesus Christ is Lord and God (Philippians 2:10-11). We believe this, and we look forward to his second coming, when he will judge the living and dead, rewarding everyone according to their deeds. He abundantly poured the gift of the Holy Spirit on us, the Spirit that promises immortality, the Spirit that makes us believers and inspires obedience. Thus, we are children of God the Father and co-heirs with Christ, whom we confess and adore, one God in a Trinity of sacred names. As he said through the prophet: "Call upon me in the day of your trial, and I will free you, and you will glorify me" (Jeremiah 29:12; Psalm 80:8). And again, he said, "Therefore it is right to reveal and confess the works of God" (Tobit 12:7).

Although I am imperfect in many things, I wish for my brothers and kinsmen to know my condition, so they can understand the desire of my soul. I do not forget the testimony of my God in the psalm: "You destroy those who speak lies" (Psalm 5:7), and again, "He who lies kills the soul" (Wisdom 1:11). And the same Lord says in the Gospel, "On the Day of Judgment, men will give account for the careless words they utter" (Matthew 12:36). Terrified and trembling, I earnestly fear judgment on that day. No one will be able to cover up or hide; all people will report their reasons for even the smallest sins before the seat of Christ, the Lord. Because of this, I have thought about writing in the past, but up until now, I have hesitated. I feared I would be attacked because I have not been educated like other people, who can combine the highest law and sacred scripture, who have never changed their speech since infancy, except to improve and to become ever more perfect.

Yet my speech and words have been translated into a foreign language, as anyone can easily determine from a taste of my writings. You can see how educated and instructed I am from my speech, because Wisdom says, "Sense and knowledge and true doctrine will be discovered through the tongue" (Sirach 4:24). But why should I make excuses, especially bold ones, next to the truth? Now in my old age, I think of what I was unable to get in my youth, because my sins opposed me and prevented me from embracing what I read. But who will believe me, even if I repeat what I said earlier? As an adolescent, almost a beardless child, I was given as a captive, before I knew what I wanted, or how I should live. That is why I blush today, and I vehemently fear exposing my ignorance, because I cannot explain it with my few words, as much as my spirit and soul rejoice. But since this opportunity has been given to me, truly, I will not be silent for fear of retribution.

And if it seems that I put myself before others, with my awkwardness and slow speaking, remember that it is written: "The blabbing tongues will quickly learn to speak peace" (Isaiah 32:4). We should reach for so much more, because we are "the letter of Christ," salvation even to the end of the earth, as it says. Even if this is not written well, I suppose it is strongly "written in your hearts, not impossible, but the Spirit of the Living God" (2 Corinthians 3:2-3). And again, the Spirit testifies: "And the country was created by the Most High" (Sirach 7:16). So first, I am an uneducated man from the country who doesn't know what to give his readers. But I certainly know that, when I was humbled earlier, I was like a rabbit that fell in deep mud.

The Powerful One came, and in his mercy, he sustained me. He raised me on high, and he placed me in the highest spot. And from there, I needed to thank him, to cry out, to repay the Lord for his great kindness, to give back something in return for his benefits. The mind of humans cannot value God benefits enough, both now and in eternity. God summoned me, the fool, from the middle of those who are seen as wise, and those who are experienced in the law, and those who are powerful in word and in every thing. And for this reason, praise God, you "great and small who fear God" (Revelation 19:5), and you who are ignorant of God's rhetoric.

So listen and examine carefully. God inspired me, even though I am surely detestable before others in this world. With fear and reverence, and without complaint, I faithfully serve the people to whom the love of Christ brought me. He gifted me in my life. If I were worthy, I would serve there truthfully and with humility.

It is necessary to make known the gift of God and eternal consolation, in the measure of faith in the Trinity, without blame. Without fear, I must faithfully expand the name of God everywhere, so that even after my death, I leave behind something valuable to the Irish, the thousands of people, my siblings and my children, who I baptized in the Lord. The Lord allowed me to be his servant, although I was not worthy or good enough. And after hardships and struggles, after my captivity, after many years, he gave me grace in that nation. In my youth, I never ever dreamed or thought of going there. But after I had arrived in Ireland, I watched sheep daily and I prayed often. More and more the love and fear of God entered me, and my faith and spirit increased, so that in a day I would say 1 to 100 prayers, and nearly as much at night. I even stayed in the woods and a mountain, and before daybreak, I rose to prayer through the snow, through the frost, through the rain. And I felt nothing bad, nor was there any laziness in me, as far as I can see, because the spirit was burning in me. There, one night in a dream, I heard a voice saying to me, "You fast well. Soon you will go to your homeland."

After a short time, I heard a response, saying to me, "Behold, your boat is prepared." But it was not near; it was around 200 miles away, in a place I had never been, a place where I knew no one.

So, after talking, I went away, leaving behind those with whom I had spent six years. I went in the virtue of the Lord, who guided my way to goodness, and I feared nothing. I reached the ship on its departure day and told the crew I had to travel with them. The captain was displeased, and he responded harshly, with indignation, "Not at all! In no way will you get to go with us." When I heard that, I left them, but soon came upon a little hut, where I stayed and prayed for the journey. After I finished the prayer, I heard someone behind me loudly exclaiming, "Come quickly, because these men call you."

I immediately went back to them, and they began to say to me, "Come! If you prove your friendship to us, we will receive you on faith. Prove your friendship however you want." Because they mentioned faith, I knew I could trust them. And although they told me they were not Christians, I truly began to hope that they would come to faith in Jesus Christ. So I gained passage with them, and we sailed straightaway.

After 3 days, we came to land, and then made a 28-day journey through the desert. The crew grew hungry and needed food, and soon the captain began to say to me, "What do you say, Christian? Your God is great and all-powerful? So why can't you pray for us, because we are starving from hunger? For it is unlikely we will see another human being again." I had told them, "Be converted to our Lord, God, from faith and from your whole heart, because nothing is impossible with him. Pray that this day he places food in your path, enough that you are satisfied, because he is full of riches everywhere." And, with God sustaining us, it was done. A herd of pigs appeared on the path before our eyes, and the crew killed many of them, staying there 2 nights, restoring themselves. Although previously they were only half-alive and forsaken, their bodies were refreshed, because they ate many pigs. Afterward, they gave highest thanks to God, and I was honored in their eyes. And from that day on, they had abundant food.

Once, they found honey in the forest and offered some to me, saying, "This must be an offering to another god." Thanks be to God, I tasted none of that honey. Still, Satan tested me. When I was sleeping that night, I felt just like a giant rock fell on me, and none of my limbs worked. I will carry that memory in this body as long as I live. I cried out in spirit like Elijah. While ill, I saw the sun rising in the sky, and with all my strength I cried, "Elijah! Elijah!" Behold, the splendor of the sun came down on me, and immediately shattered all sickness from me. And I believe that Christ my Lord (I am his servant) and his Spirit cried out on my behalf. I hope that it will be this way on the day of my distress, as the Lord says in the Gospel, "You will not be the ones who speak, but the Spirit of your Father, which speaks in you" (Matthew 10:20).

In a few years, I again was taken captive. On my first night of captivity, I heard a divine answer saying to me, "You will be with them for two months," and so it was. On the 60th night, the Lord freed me from their hands. Behold, on the way he provided us food and fire, and daily health, until we came upon men on the 14th day. As I said earlier, we made a journey through the desert for 28 days, and on that night when we came upon other people, we truly had no food.

And then, after a few years, I was in Britain with my parents, who received me as a son. And they questioned me from faith, asking that I (after undergoing such trials) never leave from them again. And there, in a dream, I clearly saw a man coming, as if from Ireland, with a countless number of letters. His name was Victor, and he gave me one of them, and I read that the start of the letter contained "voice of the Irish." And when I read aloud the start of the letter, I thought in that moment I heard voices that were by the Folcut Woods, which is by the Eastern sea. And thus they exclaimed, as if with one voice, "We beg you, holy child, that you come and walk here among us." And I was severely stung in my heart, and I was not able to read any more, and thus I was aroused. Thanks be to God, because after many years the Lord gave to them, according to their cry.

And another night, I don't know whether it was in me or next to me—God knows—I heard the most skilled words, which I could not understand until the ending of the speech: "Who lays down his soul for you." And thus, I was excited, rejoicing. And another time, I saw someone praying in me, and it was if I was inside my body, and I heard above me, that is, above my interior self. And there, the person prayed strongly with groans.

And among these I was stupefied, and I admired, and I thought, "Who is this who prays in me?" But at the end of the prayer, I was so affected that I knew it was the Spirit. And thus I awoke, and I remembered the Apostle saying, "The Spirit helps the weakness" of our prayers "for we do not know how to pray like we should, but the very Spirit prays for us with unfailing groanings" (Romans 8:26), which cannot be expressed in words. And again, "The Lord, our advocate, prays for us" (same, 34).

And once, I was tested by some of my elders who came. They put my sin up against my work as a Bishop. Surely in that day, I was greatly wounded, agitated to think that I should fall both here and in eternity. But the Lord spared the converts and the foreigners because of his good name, and he strongly came upon me in this oppression, because I did not end up in foul disgrace and reproach. I pray that God does not hold this occasion against them as a sin, for after 30 years they found me, and brought against me words which I admit I said, before I was a deacon.

Because of anxiety, with a gloomy soul, I told my best friend what I had done one day (one hour, even) in my youth, because I had not yet prevailed. I do not know, God knows, if I was 15 years old then, and I did not believe in the living God, not even when I was a child. But I remained in death and disbelief until I was strongly corrected; I was humiliated in truth, brought low by hunger and nakedness. But on the other hand, I had not willingly gone to Ireland, until I nearly died. But this was better for me, because from this I was reconciled to the Lord, and he prepared me, making me what I am today. I am now very different from what I was. I care about and have concern for the health of others, whereas back then I didn't even think about myself. So on that day when I was criticized by the people I mentioned earlier, I saw a vision at night, of writing against my face, without honor. And while this happened, I heard a divine answer, saying to me, "With misfortune, we have seen the face of the one who was chosen to expose your name." And it did not proclaim "with misfortune, you have seen" but "with misfortune, *we* have seen," as if God joined himself to me, like when he said, "Whoever touches you, touches the pupil of my eye" (Zechariah 2:8). Therefore, I give thanks to him who strengthened me in everything, so that it would not prevent me from my work and going on the path I had started, which I had learned from Christ. But rather, I sensed in me great virtue from him, and my faith was proven in the presence of God and humans.

And so, I boldly say my conscience does not condemn me,

neither now nor in the future. I have God as witness that I am not a liar in these words that I delivered to you. But rather, I grieve for my most dear friend, because we heard an accusation like this, from someone who I believed was of the same soul as me. And I learned from other brothers, before the defense, that in my absence he spoke on my behalf. I was not there. I was not in Britain or in the east. And he said to me, with his own mouth, "Look, they are giving you the rank of Bishop," of which I am not worthy. But why did he come to me, after he publicly disgraced me before everyone, the good and the bad, over something for which he had freely and happily forgiven me? It is the Lord who is greater than all things. I have said enough. But I should not hide the gift of God, which is given to us in the land of my captivity, because I searched for him steadfastly, and I found him there, and he protected me from all sins. I believe this because of his Spirit, who is working and living in me, even up to today. I would boldly repeat everything I just said. But God knows, if a man, and not the Holy Spirit, had said these things to me, perhaps I would have said nothing, because of the love of Christ.

So for this reason, I give untiring thanks to my God, because he protected me, his faithful one, on the day of my temptation, so that today I confidently offer him sacrifices. I offer my soul as a living host to my Lord Christ, who protected me from all my difficulties. And I say, "Who am I, Lord, or what is my vocation, that you have covered me with such divinity?" That's why I constantly exalt and magnify your name today among the people wherever I will go. And not just in easy times, but also in times of pressure, so that whatever happens to me, whether good or bad, I will accept it equally and always give thanks to God. God shows me that I should believe him without doubt and without end, and he has heard me, no matter how ignorant I am. So in more recent days, I set out to undertake this work which is so gracious and wonderful that I somewhat imitate those people who the Lord prophesied of old. In his Gospel, he foretold they would "bear witness to all people unto the ends of the earth." We see that this has been fulfilled. Therefore, we are witnesses, because the Gospel is proclaimed even in the farthest ends where there is no one.

My entire work is too long to explain fully, through a single writing or through multiple parts. I will not trouble my readers. Briefly, I will say how most holy God always freed me from slavery and from 12 dangers, which tested my soul, in front of many traps and things which I am not strong enough to describe with words. But now I have the Father, who knows all things, even before they are done. I am a poor little orphan, so God very often admonished me with a divine answer. How did this wisdom come to me, when it was not in me? I had not learned the number of my days, nor had I known God (Job 38:21). Where did I get the great, life-giving gift to know God or to love Him? I lost my parents and my homeland, and great burdens were offered to me, with crying and tears. And I offended people by going against the will of some of my elders, but with God's guidance, I in no way agreed or gave into them. No thanks to me, but God prevailed in me and resisted them all, so I would come to the Irish people to preach the Gospel. And in my journeys I endured attacks from nonbelievers, abusive language and many persecutions, even up to chains, and I gave up my freedom for the sake of others.

And if I am worthy, I am even ready to freely give up my soul for his name. I wish to spend my life there, up to death, if the Lord will indulge me. Because I am certainly in debt to God, who gave me such grace that many people have been reborn in God through me, and afterwards they were perfected. And priests were ordained for them everywhere, for those people who have newly come to believe, who God has taken up from the ends of the earth, just as he promised of old through the prophets: "A people comes to you from the ends of the earth, and they say, 'We have judged our fathers' idols as false, and there is no use in them' " (Jeremiah 16:19). And again, "I have set you as a light for the nations, so that you will be salvation up to the ends of the earth" (Isaiah 49:6). And there I want to await the promise of the one who never lies, as it is promised in the Gospel: "They come from the east and the west, and they recline with Abraham and Isaac and Jacob" (Matthew 8:11). We interpret this text to mean they are believers coming from the whole world.

It is fitting to fish well and diligently, as the Lord foretells, saying, "Come after me, and I will make you fishers of men" (Matthew 4:18). And again he says through the prophets, "Behold, I send many fishers and hunters, says the Lord" (Jeremiah 16:16), and others. For this reason, it is very fitting for us to cast nets, so that an abundant multitude is caught for God, that there are priests everywhere who baptize and exhort the people in need and want. As the Lord reminds and teaches, saying, "Therefore, go out, teach all nations, baptizing them in the name of the Father and the Son and the Holy Spirit. Teach them to observe all that I have ordered you. And behold, I am with you for all days, up to the end of the world" (Matthew 28:19-20). And again he says, "Therefore, go in the whole world, preach the Gospel to all creatures. Whoever believes and is baptized will be saved. Truly, whoever does not believe will be condemned" (Mark 16:15- 16). And again, "This Gospel of the Kingdom will be proclaimed to the whole world, in testimony to all people, and then the end will come" (Matthew 24:14). And again, the Lord, predicting through the prophets, says, " 'And it will be in the final days,' says the Lord, 'I will pour out my spirit upon all flesh, and your sons and your daughters will prophesy, and your children will see visions, and your elders will dream dreams. And in those days, I will pour out my Spirit even on my servants, and on my handmaids, and they will prophesy' " (Joel 2:28-29). And in Hosea, he says, "Those who are not my people, I will call them 'my people.' And mercy will follow those who mercy does not follow." (Hosea 2:24, Romans 9:25, 1 Peter 2:10). "And in the place where 'You are not my people' was said, there they will become the children of the living God" (Hosea 1:10, Romans 9:26).

But why Ireland, which never had a sign of God, other than they always revered idols and unclean things, up to now. How recently was it made the nation of God, and they were named children of God? The sons of the Scots and the daughters of kings are seen to be monks and virgins of Christ. And even one blessed Scottish woman, of noble birth, most beautiful, was an adult who I baptized. And after a few days, she came to us for this reason: She wanted us to know she had accepted a message from God. It advised her to be a virgin of Christ, and she would be close to God. Thanks be to God, on the sixth day, she most eagerly and excellently took the vows which all virgins of God do. Their parents do not let them go freely; rather, they endure persecution and false taunts from their parents, and nonetheless, their number grows larger. And we do not know the number of Christians who are born again there, along with the widows and the celibates. But the women who are held in servitude work hardest; they tirelessly persevere, even against terrors and threats. The Lord gives grace to all from his handmaids, for they still bravely imitate Christ even if they are forbidden to do so.

Even so, I have wished I could leave them and go to Britain. I was ready to leave, most eagerly, to my homeland and parents. Not only them, but I also wished to go to Gaul to visit brothers, so I may have seen the face of the saints of my God. God knows how greatly I used to wish for this, but the Spirit detains me. The Spirit testifies that if I do this, I will be marked as guilty in the future, and I fear to lose the work I have started. And it was not I, but Lord Christ who commanded me to come here, to be with these people for the rest of my life. If the Lord wanted me and protected me from all bad paths, then I should not sin before him. So I hope to do what I should, but I do not believe myself, until I leave from this body of death (Romans 7:24), because strong is the one who works daily to turn me away from faith and from a life of chastity, which I have pledged to keep until the end of my life, for my Lord Christ. But my enemy, the flesh, always drags me towards death, that is, towards enticing, forbidden deeds. And I know I have not led a perfect life, like other believers. But I confess to my Lord, and I do not blush in his sight because I am not lying. For I knew him from my youth; in me, he saw the love of God and fear of him, and until now, God willing, I have served faithfully.

Let whoever wishes laugh and insult. I will not be silent, nor will I hide the signs and miracles which to me are proof from God that he cared for me many years before they happened, as God makes all things new, even before the age of time. So I should give thanks to God without stopping, because he kindly excused my stupidity. And I give thanks that, more than once, he did not become vehemently angry with me. I was to become God's helper, according to what was shown to me and what the Spirit suggested, but I did not accept quickly. And the Lord had pity on me in thousands of thousands of ways, because he saw in me that I was prepared, but I did not know what I was doing about my state in life. Because many people prohibited this mission, and among themselves, behind my back, they talked and said, "How is it that this one sends himself into danger, among enemies who do not know the Lord?" They did not say this because they were malicious, but because they didn't understand, just as I myself have testified that I did not comprehend, because of my simplicity. I did not know the grace that was in me. Now I know what I should have done earlier.

So now, I have straight-forwardly informed my brothers and fellow servants who believed me. Because of this, I warned them and I warn you to strengthen and fortify your faith. I wish that you would imitate the greater ones and do better things. This will be my glory, because "the child's wisdom is the glory of the father"

(Proverbs 11:1, 15:20). You know, and God knows, how I was converted among you from my youth, in the faith of truth and in sincerity of heart. I lived, and I will live, the faith to them, the people I lived among. God knows I deceived none of them, nor did I think of doing so, because of God and his Church. I did not call them and us all to persecution, and the name of the Lord was not blasphemed through me, because it is written, "Woe to the one through whom the name of the Lord is blasphemed" (Leviticus 24:16). For even if I am ignorant in all things, I tried to honor anyone who served me, especially brother Christians and virgins of Christ and religious women, who voluntarily gave me little gifts from their equipment, which I blessed upon the altar and returned to them. And they were scandalized by me, wondering why I would do this. But I did this because of eternal hope. So I was on guard and took care in all things, so that the unfaithful would not seize me or the ministry of my service under some pretext. I did not want to give the unbelievers even the slightest place to defame or detract from my work.

By chance, when I baptized so many thousands of people, did I expect to receive a payment or half from one of them? Tell me what I was paid, and I will return it to you. When I ordained priests through my poverty and ministry, I gave it to them for free. If I requested money from any one of them, even as little as the price of my shoes, tell me. Speak against me, and I will return it to you. I have spent more for you, so much that it seizes me. I proceeded among you and everywhere for your sake, in many dangers, even to foreign lands where no one lives beyond, and where nobody had come. Nobody baptized, or ordained priests, or perfected the people. I gave to the Lord, diligently and most freely; I did it all for your health. Sometimes, I gave gifts to kings, because I paid wages to their sons who walked with me, so no one would seize me with my companions. One day, they most eagerly desired to kill me, but my time had not yet come. They took everything which they found in our possession, and I was captured with chains. And on the 14th day, the Lord freed me from their power; and whatever was ours, it was returned to us, because of God and the close friends who we provided for earlier.

You are aware of how much I spent on them, the ones who are judges in all areas that I visited most often. For I estimate I gave a price no less than 15 men to them. I did this so you might delight in me, as I always delight in you with God. I do not regret it, nor am I finished. I still spend and I will spend more. Powerful is the Lord who presently allows me to "spend myself for your souls" (2 Corinthians 12:15). Behold, I call upon God's witness in my soul, because I do not lie. I have not composed this for you, so it would be a cause of flattery or greed, nor do I hope for your honor. For the honor that is not seen, but is believed by the heart, is enough for me, because faithful is the one who promises, who never lies. But now I see in the present age that I have been lifted up by the Lord higher than I expected. And I was not worthy, nor was I such a distinguished person that this elevation befits me. I know most certainly that poverty and misfortune suit me better than delicacy and riches. But even Christ the Lord was a pauper for our sake. Truly, I am miserable and unhappy, and if I wanted riches, which I don't have now, I do not judge myself worthy of them, because every day I expect to be exterminated or surrounded or forced into slavery or something like that. But I fear none of these things, because of the promise of the heavens, because I have thrown myself in the hand of the all-powerful God who rules everywhere, as the prophet says, "Throw your thoughts on God, and he will nourish you" (Psalm 64:23).

Behold, now I commend my soul to my most faithful God, for whom I work as an ambassador in my obscurity (2 Corinthians 5:20). But because he does not accept people based on their rank, he chose me for this office, so that I might be one of his least servants. "So how shall I repay Him for all the things that he paid to me?" (Psalm 115:12). But what will I say, or what can I promise to my Lord? Because I can do nothing, unless he has given it to me. But he searches the heart and mind, because I fully and greatly desire, and I am prepared should he give me his chalice to drink, just as he indulged others who love him. For this reason, let it not seize me from my God, that I ever lose his people who I acquired in the ends of the earth. I pray to God that he gives me perseverance, and he deems it worthy that I return to him as a faithful witness, up to my passing away, because of my God. And if I ever faked any of the goodness because of my God whom I love, I beg that he let me pour out my blood with those foreigners and captives for the sake of his name, even if I would be deprived of a burial, or my most wretched corpse would be divided into pieces by dogs or harsh beasts, or the vultures of the sky ate it. Most certainly, I think if this happened to me, I will have gained my soul with my body, because without any doubt on that day we are resurrected in the clarity of the sun, that is, in the glory of Christ Jesus our redeemer, Son of the Living God, and "co-heirs with Christ" (Romans 8:17), "and conformed to his future image" (Romans 8:29), because from him and through him and in him, we will reign.

For that sun we see, God willing, rises for us every day, but it never reigns, and its splendor does not remain. But all who worship the sun will wickedly come to a wretched punishment. For we believe in and worship the true Sun, Christ who will never die. And whoever does his will shall not perish, but shall remain in eternity, just as Christ remains in eternity, who reigns with God the all-powerful Father and with the Holy Spirit, before time, and now, and through all time, forever and ever. Amen.

Look, again and again, I briefly put forth these words *of my confession*. I testify in truth and rejoicing of heart, before God and his holy angels, that I never had any reason, other than the Gospel and its promises, to ever return to those people who I had escaped from earlier. But I entreat those who believe and fear God, whoever will deign to look at or receive this writing. Patrick, a sinner, obviously untaught, wrote this in Ireland. May no one ever say that my ignorance is the cause, if I did or showed any small thing which pleases God. But rather, judge for yourselves and believe most truly, that it was a gift from God. And this is my confession before I die.

Letter to Coroticus[1]

I am Patrick, an ignorant sinner, as you may know. I confess that I have been appointed a Bishop in Ireland. I most certainly believe that I have accepted all that I am from God. Thus, I live among foreigners, like a stranger and an exile, out of love of God. He is the witness to this. It is not that I wanted such long and harsh words to pour forth from my mouth, but I am driven by zeal for God and the truth of Christ, who has called me to love of neighbors and children. For their sake, I gave up my homeland and my parents and my soul, even until death, if I am worthy.

I have sworn a vow to my God to instruct people, even if I am despised by those who I have written to with my hand. And I composed these words. I gave and delivered them to soldiers, to be sent to Coroticus. I do not speak to my people, nor the people of holy Rome, but I speak to the people of demons. Because of their evil works, I treat them as enemies. The companions of the Scottish and Pictish rebels live in death, as they want to feast on the blood of numberless innocent Christians, who I brought to God and confirmed in Christ.

The day after I confirmed the newly baptized in white garments, while the oil of faith still shined on their foreheads, they were cruelly butchered and slaughtered with swords by the people I mentioned earlier.

I sent a letter with priests and a holy elder, whom I had taught from infancy, to beg them to return some of the plunder or the captive baptized whom they had captured. The only thing they gave them was laughter. So I don't know what I lament more: those who were killed, those who were captured, or those who the devil boldly ensnares, because they will be delivered with him for an equal, everlasting punishment in hell. Whoever makes sin is the servant of sin (1 John 3:8) and is called the child of the devil.

For this reason, let every God-fearing man know that they are alien to me and to Christ, my Lord. I act as an ambassador on his behalf. He says people who kill fathers and murder brothers are like violent wolves, "devouring the people of God, as if they were eating bread" (Psalm 13:4). "The unjust have demolished your law, Lord" (Psalm 118:126), which, by the will of God, was planted and taught

---

[1] Coroticus is a king who captured and enslaved some newly-baptized Irish, which prompted Saint Patrick to write this strong condemnation.

in Ireland, abundantly and well, in former times.

I do not force myself in, where I don't belong. I have a part with those whom he called and predestined to preach the Gospel to the ends of the earth, even in large persecutions. I do not care if the tyrant Coroticus hates me as an enemy. He neither respects God, nor God's priests whom he chose and granted the highest, most divine, most exalted power: "What they bind on earth will also be bound in heaven" (Matthew 18:18).

Therefore, I very much pray to the holy and humble of heart. It is not lawful to fawn over these murderers, to take up food and drink with them, or to receive alms from them. Not until they do penance to satisfy God, a penance so harsh that their tears flow forth, and not until they free the servants of God and the baptized helpers of Christ, who died and was crucified for them.

"The Most High rejects the gifts of sinners. A wealthy person who offers a poor sacrifice is like a person who sacrifices a son in the sight of his father" (Sirach 34:19-20). "Riches," it says, "which were unjustly gathered will be vomited from his belly. The angel of death draws him. He will be punished with the anger of dragons. He will be destroyed by the serpent's tongue" (Job 20:15- 16). That is, everlasting fire consumes him.

And in the same way, woe to the man who fills up on things that aren't his. "How does it benefit a man, when he gains the whole world and loses his soul?" (Matthew 16:26). It is tedious to discuss or make known every example, to pick through the entire law to find testimony about such greed. Greed is a deadly sin. "You will not desire your neighbor's things. You will not kill." (Exodus 20:17, 13). A killer cannot be with Christ. "Whoever hates their brother is considered a murderer," or "Whoever does not love their brother stays in death" (1 John 3:14,15). How much more guilty is the person who befouls their hands in the blood of the children of God? God acquired these children, not too long ago, in this distant land, through the encouragement of my littleness.

Did I come to Ireland without God, or according to the flesh? What drew me here? I am bound by the spirit to remain here, to never return home to see my relatives again. Through gentle mercy, I do works for those people who once kidnapped me, and who devastated the servants and maids of my father's house. According to the flesh, I was a freeborn; I was born to a decurion father. But I have sold my nobility for the sake of helping others. I do not blush, nor am I ashamed of what I have done. For I am a servant in Jesus Christ, our Lord, in a land where they do not know me.

"A prophet does not have honor in his own land" (Mark 6:4). We are surely not from one flock, and we do not have one God as father. As he says, "Whoever is not with me is against me, and whoever does not gather with me separates" (Luke 11:23). He is a separator; he does not gather. "One destroys, another builds" (Sirach 34:28). I do not want what is mine.

I'm not doing this for my own sake, but truly, God gave this duty in my heart, so that, in these days, I would be one of the hunters or fishers who God foretold (Jeremiah 16:16). I am hated. What will I do, Lord? I am deeply despised. Behold, your sheep are ripped into pieces around me. They are in the hands of the Scots and Picts, driven away by arrogant robbers, commanded by the hostile-minded Coroticus. A betrayer of Christians is far from the love of God.

Greedy wolves glut themselves on the flock of the Lord, which grew well in Ireland, strengthened with great care. And the sons of the Scots and the daughters of the chieftains became monks and virgins of Christ. There were so many, I cannot number them. "Do not be pleased by injuries to the just, for even to hell, it will not please" (Sirach 9:17).

Who of the saints would not be horrified to eat food and laugh with such people? They fill up their houses with the spoils of dead Christians. They live like robbers, ignorant of their wretchedness. They drink poison; they extend a lethal drink to their friends and family. Just as Eve did not know what death she handed to her husband, so are all who do evil. They work for eternal death and everlasting punishment.

The custom of Roman and Gallic Christians is this. They send holy, capable men to the Franks and other peoples, with many thousands of soldiers, for redeeming the captive baptized. But you kill them all, and you sell them to a foreign people, ignorant of God. You trade the members of Christ like you're in a whorehouse. What sort of hope do you have in God?

God will judge whoever agrees with you, or whoever speaks to you with flattery and strange words. For it is written, "Not only the evildoers, but also those who agree with them, are damned" (Romans 1:32). I do not know what I will say, or how I will speak any more, about the dead children of God. The sword has beaten them, unfeelingly and excessively. For it is written, "Weep with those who weep" (Romans 12:15). And again, "If one member is in pain, all members suffer" (1 Corinthians 12:26).

For this reason, the Church bemoans and laments her sons and daughters whom the sword has not yet killed, but who are taken and sent away to far distant lands, where sin openly oppresses, where sin shamelessly lives and thrives. There, freeborn Christian people are put up for sale. They are driven back to slavery, especially to the lowest, worst and most wicked rebels of the Picts.

For this reason, with sadness and mourning, I cry aloud, "O most beautiful and beloved brothers and children who I bore in Christ! I cannot count how many of you there are!" I am not worthy to serve God or humans. The injustice of hostile enemies has prevailed over us, and it is as if we have become foreigners.

Clearly, they don't believe in the one baptism that we have, nor do they believe that we have one God as father. To them, it is an indignity that we are from Ireland. As it is said, "Do you not have one God? Why does each one of you abandon your neighbors?" (Malachi 2:10)

For this reason, I grieve for you. You are most dear to me, and I grieve for you. But again, I rejoice within myself. I did not labor in vain, and my journey was not empty. Wickedness has brought such unutterable horrors, true, but I give thanks to God, believing that all of you, who I baptized in this world, have gone away to paradise. I know you have begun migrating to the place where "there will be neither night, nor day, nor any more death" (Revelation 21:4). You will rejoice like bulls who have been released from their chains; you will crush the unjust, and they will be ashes under your feet.

Therefore, you will rule with the apostles and prophets and martyrs, and you will hold endless kingship, just as he himself has testified (to the one who asked): "They will come from the East and the West, and they will recline with Abraham and Isaac and Jacob in the kingdom of Heaven" (Matthew 8:11). "The dogs and the sorcerers and murderers and liars are outside" (Revelation 22:15). As for those who break oaths, "their portion is in the eternal lake of fire" (Revelation 21:8). There is a reason the Apostle said, "When the just person will be saved with difficulty, where will the sinner and unholy breaker of the law find themselves?" (1 Peter 4:18).

As for Coroticus and his most wicked rebels against Christ, where will they see themselves? They distribute baptized working girls and orphans' farms among their most foul assistants, all for the sake of a miserable, temporary kingdom that will pass by in a moment like clouds, or scatted apart by the wind like smoke. In this way, sinners and deceivers will perish from the face of the Lord. Then, the just will feast in great harmony with Christ. They will judge the nations and will rule over evil kings forever and ever. Amen.

I openly testify to God and his angels that it will be so, in the way God has announced to me in my ignorance. I am not using my own words (which I am writing in Latin), but the words of God and the apostles and the prophets, who are never false: "Whoever will believe will be saved; truly, whoever does not believe will be condemned" (Mark 16:16). God has spoken.

Whatever servant of God carries this letter, I earnestly pray that they will do so publicly, and that they will not hide the letter from anyone. It would be better if the letter is read openly, before the whole community and before Coroticus.

If God inspires them, they will then return to their senses and to God. At this late hour, they will repent that they have so wickedly committed murder against the brothers of the Lord, and they will free the captive baptized who they captured earlier. By doing so, they will deserve to live in God, and they will be made whole here and in eternity. Peace be to the Father, and to the Son and to the Holy Spirit. Amen.

Synod of the Bishops Patrick, Gallagher and Iser

We give thanks to God, the Father and the Son and the Holy Spirit. To the priests and deacons and all clergy, greetings from the Bishops Patrick, Gallagher and Iser[2].

Rather than blame people for what they have done, we are sending this to warn the negligent. As Solomon says, "It is better to rebuke than to get angry" (Sirach 20:2). Copies of our decree are written below, and they begin like this:

1. If anyone has attempted to ransom captives in the community, without permission and by himself, he deserves to be excommunicated.

2. Lectors should become thoroughly acquainted with the church in which they sing.

3. A wandering priest is not allowed in the community.

4. If someone has received permission and collected money, he shall not take more than what he needs.

5. If anything is left over, he shall put it upon the Bishop's altar, and it will be given to others in need.

6. Whatever kind of clergyman, from a porter up to a priest, who is seen without a tunic and does not cover up his foul belly or his nakedness, and if his hair is not trimmed in the Roman fashion, and his wife walks around with her head uncovered, let them be equally condemned by the laity and separated from the church.

7. When a priest is ordered to pray morning or evening prayer and he neglects his duty, let him be treated like an alien, unless he was prevented from praying by the heavy yoke of slavery.

---

[2] The Latin names are Patricius, Auxilius and Isserninus

8. If a priest has given a pledge of any size to a pagan person, and if he has been cheated through some trick (which isn't surprising), that pagan has deceived the priest out of his own things. The priest should be released from the debt. And if he fights against the man with weapons, he deserves to be considered outside of the Church.

9. A monk and a virgin, him from one place and her from another, shall not both stay in the same guest chamber, nor should they ride in one chariot from village to village, nor should they talk intimately with each other.

10. If a lector has proven himself good at singing psalms, and he lets his hair grow wild, he should be excluded from the church, unless he returns himself to his former state.

11. If any priest has been excommunicated by someone, and another person supported him, both should undergo an equal punishment.

12. If any Christian has been excommunicated, not even his alms should be received.

13. Alms offered in the church by pagans are not allowed to be received.

14. A Christian who has killed or fornicated or gone to a fortune-teller like a pagan should serve a year of penance for each crime. When it is done, let him come with witnesses to the year of penance, and afterwards he will be absolved by a priest.

15. Let he who has committed theft be punished for half a year, including 20 days with bread; if it can be done, he must pay for the stolen items. In this way, he will be restored to the Church.

16. Let a curse come upon the Christian who believes in a lamia (which is defined as "witch" or "vampire") or who prizes a false legend more than souls. Let them not be received into the church until they once more renounce the crime they have committed, and let them serve penance with great care.

17. A virgin who has sworn a vow of chastity to God and who later marries a husband in the flesh should be excommunicated until she is converted. If she undergoes conversion and has renounced the adultery, let her serve penance, and afterwards, they should not sleep in the same bed or stay in the same household.

18. If anyone has been excommunicated, they should not enter a church on Easter night unless they have taken up a penance.

19. If a Christian woman has accepted a man in an honest marriage and a little later is divorced from the first man and joins herself to another in adultery, let her be excommunicated.

20. A Christian who cheats on any debt, in the manner of the pagans, should be excommunicated until the debt is paid.

21. If a Christian is abandoned by someone and calls them to court, not to the church, to have the case examined, they should be treated like an alien.

22. If a father hands over his daughter to a man in an honest marriage, and she loves another man, and the father agrees with his daughter and accepts a dowry from the second man, both should be excluded from the church.

23. If a priest builds a church, whoever he is, he shall not offer mass there before bringing his bishop to consecrate it, as it is fitting for bishops to do so.

24. If any stranger has come to a place, he shall not baptize nor offer mass, nor consecrate, nor build a church until he has received permission from the local bishop. For whoever has permission from pagans should be treated like an alien.

25. If religious people offer gifts on a day when the bishop is in a particular church, they will be considered bishop gifts, according to the ancient custom that pertains to bishops. He can use the gifts as he sees fit, whether to purchase necessary things or to give to the needy.

26. If a priest truly goes against his bishop and seizes the bishop gifts, he will be separated from the church because of his filthy desire for wealth.

27. A priest who is at the same place as the bishop is not allowed to baptize or to offer mass or take control of anything, no matter how long he has been there, and if this is not done, let him be excommunicated.

28. If a priest was excommunicated, let him do his prayers alone, not in the same house with others. He is not allowed to offer mass or consecrate things until he has been corrected by punishment. He who does not act in this way should be punished twice.

29. If one of the brothers wishes to accept the grace of God, he should not be baptized before he undergoes a 40-day fast.

30. A bishop, no matter who he is, who goes into another diocese should not dare to ordain a man unless he has received permission from the local bishop. On the Lord's Day, he will offer mass under the same conditions, and he will be happy to obey.

31. If two priests have come to fight because of some disagreement, and one of the two hires an assassin for killing his enemy, this is rightly called "homicide." This priest shall be treated as alien by all good people.

32. If any one of the priests wishes to help a captive, let him go to the captors with his own money. For if he causes harm by means of robbery, many priests will be reviled because of one thief. Let the priest who does this be excommunicated.

33. A priest who comes to us from Britain without a letter of introduction from his bishop, even if he lives in community with others, will not be allowed to minister.

Similarly, a deacon who comes to us without consulting his abbot, or who acts in another diocese without a letter of introduction, should not be allowed to serve food. He should be delivered to the priest he defied, for penance. And a monk who wanders without permission should be returned to his abbot.

The rules of the synod end here.

Some Proverbs of Saint Patrick

Patrick says: It is more beneficial for us to warn negligent people, lest they drown in abundant delights, than it is to blame them for what they have done. Solomon: *It is better to admonish than to lose one's temper* (Sirach 20:2).

Patrick says: It is not proper for judges of the church to have the fear of men, but the fear of God, because *Fear of God is the beginning of wisdom* (Psalm 111:10).

It is not proper for judges of the church of God to have the wisdom of this world, because "the wisdom of this world is foolishness before God" (1 Corinthians 3:19). Rather, they should have the wisdom of God.

It is not proper for judges of the church to receive bribes, "because bribes blind the eyes of the wise, and they change the words of the just" (Deuteronomy 16:19).

It is not proper for judges of the church to show favor in judgment due to a person's reputation: "There is no regard for a person's reputation before God" (Romans 2:11).

It is not proper for judges of the church to have worldly concerns, but they should follow the divine model, because it is not proper for the servant of God to be cautious or shrewd (Luke 16:8).

It is not proper for judges of the church to be overly swift in judgment until they know the truth of what is written: "Do not wish for a judge to be very quick" (Proverbs 25:8).

It is not proper for judges of the church to be fickle (James 1:19-20).

It is not proper for judges of the church to speak lies, because a lie is a great crime (John 8:44). But it is proper for judges of the church to render right judgment, because they will be judged by the measure with which they have judged (Matthew 7:2).

Patrick says: Eagerly follow the example of very great people, where you will find nothing of falsehood (John 18:38).

Patrick says: Judges who do not correctly proclaim the judgments of the church are not judges, but frauds (Daniel 13:5-9).

Canons Written by Saint Patrick

1. On the judgment of priests, so they will not be like the unjust or like the infidels.

The person who is wise in all worldly things, if he is wise, should not judge the judgments of the Church.

2. On the subjection of the people to a ruler.

You are servants, and you should be anxious about your rulers whom you assist and serve, whoever they may be.

3. On the penance of blaspheming the principal good.

Whoever mutters words of blasphemy against the principal good, through hate or envy, let his penance be bread and water for seven days, following the example of Miriam murmuring against Moses.

4. On that which is uncertain, whether a bishop, after lapsing, can be returned to his former position.

He who sins while he is a bishop should be excommunicated, because great is the dignity of that name; nonetheless, it is possible to redeem one's soul, after penance, and to go to a former position with much difficulty. I don't know whether it can be done. God knows.

5. On receiving adulterers after penance, and on the amount of penance necessary for adulterers.

If any woman has committed adultery with another man, he will not marry another woman while the first woman is still living. If she is powerfully converted and undergoes penance, he will support her, and she will serve him like a servant, and let the penance be bread and water for the duration of an entire year during which the two should not stay in one bed.

6. On submitting a foreigner to judgment.

If any questions arise on this island, let them be referred to the apostolic chair.

7. On giving penance to someone on their last breath.

If anyone is weakened by infirmity, they should still undergo penance out of necessity, because God is merciful.

8. On how the foolish should not be leaders.

The synod of the whole world, and Patrick, have decreed: Whoever is foolish is in no way permitted to be in charge. Rather, the fool should do his work under the hand of a Catholic abbot or father.

9. On collecting money out of necessity, so as not to receive censure.

Patrick says: If someone has received the permission of the bishop to hold a collection for the ransom of a captive, they should not request more money than necessary. If something extra is left over, let it be placed upon the altar, and let it be given to the needy and the captives.

The same applies if someone has collected money under the name of mercy. Let him not dare to rob the church of God, whether he is a king or a commoner, for it is better to give money than to conceal it.

Part 2

Texts Attributed to Saint Patrick

Synod Attributed to Saint Patrick

1. On living with brothers who are sinners.

For what you have commanded about living with brothers who are sinners, listen to the Apostle saying, "Do not share food with such a person" (1 Corinthians 5:11). Do not eat a dish with him. Again, if you are an ox and you are threshing, that is, if you are a teacher and you teach, "The ox should not be muzzled" (1 Corinthians 9:9), and "Worthy is your payment" (Luke 10:7). But "Do not let the oil of sinners fatten your head" (Psalm 140:5); instead, snatch it up and make it known.

2. On their offerings.

"Your roof and your food are enough." Again, "Refuse the gifts of the wicked" (Sirach 34:23), because that is like feeding bad fuel to a lamp.

3. On the punishment after a ruin.

It is established that an abbot sees who is given the power of binding and dissolving punishments, but forgiveness is more fitting, following the example of the Scriptures. If a punishment is truly undertaken with crying and wailing and the clothing of mourning, it will be a brief punishment rather than a long one, and the penitent will be forgiven with moderation.

4. On rejecting an excommunicated person.

Hear the Lord, saying, "If you do not hear, then may you be like the Gentiles and tax collectors" (Matthew 18:37). Do not curse, but reject an excommunicated person from communion and the table and mass and peace. And, "If he is a heretic, shun him after giving him one warning" (Titus 3:10).

5. On suspicious motives.

Listen to the Lord, saying, "Allow them to grow together until the harvest" (Matthew 13:30), that is, until that day when he will come and "will reveal the intentions of the heart" (1 Corinthians 4:5). Do not make a judgment before the day of judgment. Look at Judas, who regularly ate at the table of the Lord, and look at the thief in paradise.

6. On the punishment of the Church.

Again, hear the Lord saying, "He who pours out [innocent] blood, let his own blood be shed" (Genesis 9:6), but the one who carries the sword is said to be held innocent of punishment. But otherwise, the Gospel law says, "From the one who takes what is yours, do not take it back" (Luke 6:30) but give it freely; if he returns it, receive it humbly.

7. On uncertain baptisms.

It stands that those who accept the symbol of tradition from someone should not be rebaptized, because the sin of the sower does not stain the seed. But truly, this is not rebaptism, but baptism. And we do not believe those who have lapsed from the faith are absolved, unless I have accepted them through the imposition of hands.

8. On excommunication from the Church.

The Church is not made for defending things, but for persuading someone to judgment, so that those who flee towards the bosom of Mother Church will die a spiritual death.

(9 is missing.)

10. On falling, after being raised to a higher position.

Hear the rules that have been put in place: If a man with a position falls, let him rise without his position. Let him be content with his name and dismissed from ministry, if he does not withdraw after sinning in the sight of God in this way.

11. On separating by gender, after falling.

Let the one who has sinned examine himself in his conscience, to see if his love and desire of sin have stopped, because a dead body does not infect another dead body. If the desires have not stopped, let them be separated.

12. On offerings for the sake of the dead.

Hear the Apostle saying, "Therefore, there is sin that leads to death. I do not say that you should pray for someone who commits those sins" (1 John 5:16). And the Lord: "Do not give holy things to dogs" (Matthew 7:6). For if a person does not deserve to accept sacrifice while alive, how will it help after his or her death?

13. On sacrifice.

On Easter night, even if it is possible to carry it outside, don't carry it outside, but offer it to the faithful. What else could "the lamb is taken in one household" (Exodus 12:3) mean, other than Christ is believed and received under one faith?

14. On abstaining from drink.

It stands that Christ made no new laws about fasting, while coming to fulfill the covenant. Therefore, what is different between the Novatians[1] and Christians, except that the Novatian never stops abstaining, and the Christian abstains only for a time. The Christian takes place and time and person into account, through all circumstances.

---

[1] The Novatians were a group of Christians who believed it was immoral to drink wine in the morning, among other things.

15. On teaching or leaving a country.

First, a person should teach their home country, following the example of the Lord. And if it is not successful, they should leave afterward, following the example of the Apostle. But whoever can succeed is allowed to be tested; they can teach and show themselves everywhere. The person who truly cannot do this should be quiet and go away. Surely, one person is sent by Jesus to his own house, while another person is told to follow.

16. On false bishops.

He who is not picked by another bishop, following the apostolic succession, is damned. And furthermore, he is to be shunned and degraded by the rest of the people.

17. On the purpose of monks.

There are monks who live by themselves without earthly support, under the power of a bishop or an abbot. However, they are not monks, but aimless people, full of contempt for the world. Each one, for the perfect life, from the perfect age (that is, 20 years), should be compelled not to witness, but to fulfill their vow, so that it is "as if your own heart has been placed before you" (1 Corinthians 7:37). Also, so that, "I will give my vow in the sight of the Lord" (Psalm 65:14, 18). And further, the place constrains what kind of vow is lived, if superabundance is to be shunned in all things in life, because they are called in coldness and nakedness, in hunger and thirst, in vigils and in fasting. (2 Corinthians 11:27)

18. On three seeds of the Gospels.

"Some seed fell on rich soil, and produced fruit, a hundred or sixty or thirtyfold" (Matthew 13:8, 25). The hundredth are bishops and doctors, who are all things to all people. The sixtieth are priests and widows who are chaste. The thirtieth are laity who are faithful, who believe perfectly in the Trinity. This is not larger in the harvest of the Lord; truly, we combine monks and virgins with the hundredth.

19. What day is for baptizing.

They are catechumens eight days. Afterwards, they are baptized on a solemnity of the Lord, that is, Easter, Pentecost and Epiphany.

20. On parishes.

One should not speak with monks whose evil is unheard of. We truly and suitably take up unity among the people.

21. On retaining and dismissing monks.

One should perform his tasks in the church in which he has been trained, unless a greater reason arises for him to be taken to a far place, with the permission of the abbot. If he has really left for a good reason, the blessing, "Behold the Lamb of God," is said, because he is not one of the ones who seeks his own will, but that of "Jesus Christ" (Philippians 2:21). However, they should not let the lower monks run around on the pretext of a calling.

22. On receiving the Eucharist, after falling

The Eucharist is received, after a consideration of the prison. This matters most on Easter Night, on which the person who does not receive the Eucharist is not faithful. Therefore, the time for them is short and limited, lest the soul of the faithful is lost in this time, spent hungering for healing. As the Lord says, "If you will not eat the flesh of the Son of Man, you will not have life in you" (John 6:54).

23. On oaths.

"Do not swear oaths at all" (Matthew 5:34). As a result of this reading, Jesus teaches not to swear to another creature. Swear to nothing but the Creator, as is the way of the prophets: "The Lord lives and my soul lives" (1 Samuel 25:26) and, "The Lord lives, who I assist today" (1 Kings 18:15). Therefore, the end of arguments is nothing but the Lord. Let a man swear by all that he loves.

24. On a dispute between two people, without witnesses.

It stands that whoever is being tried should testify through the four holy Gospels, before they receive communion, and then, the report is allowed, under judgment.

25. On marriage to the spouse of a dead brother.

Listen to the decrees of the synod over and above the others. The death of a brother does not rise above a marriage. As the Lord says, "They were two in one flesh" (Genesis 2:24). Therefore, the wife of a brother is your sister.

26. On marrying a prostitute.

Hear the Lord saying, "Whoever is joined to a prostitute becomes one body with her" (1 Corinthians 6:16). Again: "Adulterers should be stoned" (Leviticus 20:10; Deuteronomy 22:22); that is, they should die in this life in order to stop strengthening the things that encourage adultery. Again: "If a woman has committed adultery, can she not return to her former husband?" (Jeremiah 3:1). Again: It is not allowed for a man to dismiss his wife "except in the case of adultery" (Matthew 5:32, 19:9), and if it is said, for this reason. And they are not forbidden from marrying another, just like after the death of the first spouse.

27. On the will of a woman or a father, in marriage.

Let the woman do whatever the father wants, because "the man is the head of his wife" (1 Corinthians 9:3). But the father should seek the will of the woman, since "God leaves humans in the hands of their counsel" (Sirach 15:14).

28. On a first or a second vow.

The first vows and first marriage are observed in the same way. The second vows do not invalidate the first, unless there was adultery.

29. On marrying a relative.

Understand what the law says, nothing more, nothing less. Therefore, we observe what is before us: the couple to be married must be separated by four generations. A marriage between more closely related people is not to be seen or heard.

30. On restoring customs.

What isn't forbidden is allowed. Truly, the laws of the jubilee (that is, 50 years) are observed, which were not affirmed in older, more uncertain times. And therefore, all business under the Romans is confirmed.

31. On people who believe before baptism, how they undergo penance.

The sins of all are forgiven in baptism. The sinner is judged faithful, because he lived with a faithful conscience in an unfaithful time.

The synod of Patrick ends.

Other Canons Attributed to Saint Patrick
From the codex of the Benedictine College in Cambridge

1. On the unity of substitutes.

Now, who dares to separate unity, which no man can take apart or lay hands on? "Then the group of believers were of one heart and one soul, and nothing separated them, and nobody claimed his possessions were his own, but all things were held in common. Also, grace was great above them all, and no one among them was needy. For whoever owned lands or houses sold them to buyers, and they put the payment before [the feet of] the apostles, and it was divided to each person according to his need." (Acts 4:32-35). Afterwards: "Then there was a certain man, named Ananias," and so on, up to those words: "Then, hearing these words, Ananias fell down and died." (Acts 5:1-5).

2. On theft done in church.

He who has stolen money from the holy church, where martyrs and the bodies of saints live, let his hand or foot be cut off, or let him be thrown in jail, or let him be thrown out in wandering, and let him repay double. And he will be judged unable to return until he has filled up his punishment.

3. On true widows.

Concerning true widows, Paul says: "Let a widow be chosen, no less than 60 years old, the woman of one man" (1 Timothy 5:9). Note: If she has had many men [that is, she has been married many times], she is not a widow.

Then, there are two following canons close by, but the Benedictine manuscript doesn't say whether they are from Saint Patrick or another author. The second one is also in the Cottoniano codex of canons, titled 66, and it is treated as ascribed to an Irish synod.

1. On that which is not grounds for divorce: If she is sterile, if she is deformed, if she is old, if she is smelly, if she is a drunk, if she is prone to anger, if she is quarrelsome, then the marriage holds, whether you like it or not. Whatever type of person is accepted in marriage, that person is held in marriage.

2. Every adulterer is excluded from praise and communion of the altar, from correspondence or from attendance at mass, until they do penance.

Charter of Saint Patrick.

(Most believe this was written by a Welsh monk, not Saint Patrick.)

In the name of our Lord, Jesus Christ. I, Patrick, the humble servant of God, in the year of his incarnation 425, in Ireland after being sent by the Holy Father, Pope Celestine, give thanks to God because I have converted the Irish to the way of truth. And having been united with them in the Catholic faith, at length I have returned to Britain, and, as I believe, led by God, "who is the way and the life" (John 14:6), I have entered the island Ynswytryn, in which I have found a holy and ancient place, chosen and sanctified by God, in honor of the undefiled Virgin Mary, mother of God.

In that place, I have discovered some brothers imbued with the rudiments of the Catholic faith and pious conversation, who follow the disciples of Saints Fagan and Damian[1], whose names I truly believe "are written in heaven" (Philippians 4:3) because of the merits of their lives. And because "the just will be remembered forever" (Psalm 112:6), I have been delighted to keep their memory with these brothers, whose names I wish to collect in my writing, which are: Brumban, Hyregaan, Bremwal, Wencreth, Bantommeweng, Adelwolred, Loyor, Wellias, Breden, Swelwes, Hinloernus, and another Hyn.

These men have been descended from noble birth and, desiring to ornament the nobility of their faith with works, they have decided to lead a hermit's life. And because I have found them to be humble and quiet, I have decided it would be better to stay with them than to live in royal courts (Psalm 84:10). But because all of them "were one heart and one mind" (Acts 4:32), we chose to all live together, and to eat and drink at the same time, and to sleep in the same house. They offered to let me stay with them in this way, despite my reluctance. "For I am not worthy to loosen the straps of their sandals" (Mark 1:7).

And while we were leading the monastic life in this way, according to the commendable rule of the Fathers, the brothers showed to me the writings of Saints Fagan and Damian as a prayer offering. They were composed of how 12 disciples of Saints Philip and James built that ancient church in honor of the Virgin Mary, our

---

[1] The names in Latin are Phagani and Diruviani.

42

pre-consecrated Advocate, through the teaching of the blessed archangel Gabriel, and moreover, how the Lord had dedicated that heavenly church in honor of his Mother, and how three pagan kings gave to those 12 disciples 12 portions of land for their sustenance. Moreover, I have found, even in more recent writings, how Saints Fagan and Damian received 30 years' indulgence from Pope Eleutherius, who had sent them. And I, brother Patrick, have only acquired 12 years of indulgence in my time from Pope Celestine of holy memory.

After much time, having taken the Welsh with me as my brothers, through the dense forest with great difficulty, we climbed to the top of a mountain that stands out on that island. When we arrived there, one old and almost destroyed temple became visible. Despite its state, it was suitable for the devotion of Christians, and (it seemed to me) chosen by God.

When we had gone down there, we were filled with such a sweet odor that we thought we had been placed in the loveliness of Paradise. Then, going forward and back, diligently searching the place, we found one volume in which was written the Acts of the Apostles, together with the acts and achievements of Saints Fagan and Damian. For the most part, the book was destroyed, but at the end of the volume, we found writing that said what Fagan and Damian predicted, through a revelation of our Lord, Jesus Christ, at that temple which they built in honor of Saint Michael, the Archangel. They built the temple so he would have honor from men there, and in order to introduce the people to him, who is held in perpetual honor by humans, as commanded by God.

And after those writings had delighted us, we kneeled while reading the ending out loud. For those writings said that the venerable Fagan and Damian paused there for nine years, and that they even received an indulgence of 30 years for all worshippers of Christ with pious inclination who visited that place for the honor of Blessed Michael. Therefore, having found such a great treasure of divine goodness, I and my Welsh brothers fasted for three months; we were empty, and with vigilant prayer we commanded the demons and various beasts that appeared.

Moreover, on a certain night, when I had surrendered myself to sleep, the Lord Jesus appeared to me in a vision, saying: "Patrick, my servant, you know I have chosen this place for the honor of my name, that here people may invoke my helper, the archangel

Michael. And I give this as a sign to you and your brothers that they also may believe: Your left forearm will wither until you announce what you have seen to your brothers in the lower cells, and there you will return to normal."

And thus it was.

From that day, we placed two brothers there in perpetuity, lest future pastors make decisions from anything other than a just cause. Further, because of my encouragement, Arnulph and Ogmar, Irish brothers who had come with me from Ireland, undertook to remain there, saying prayers humbly. I entrusted the pages to them in person, retaining another copy in the ark of Holy Mary, as a monument for the future.

I believe it will be as the prophet foretold on the mountain: People from all parts will come to the woods with axes and hatchets (Psalm 74:6), destroying them with pious intention, so that the approach of Christians may be prepared more easily as they visit the church of the kind Blessed and Ever Virgin Mary. And I, brother Patrick, through the counsel of my brothers, now take my leave after 100 days of grace.

The Book of Three Dwelling Places
Attributed to Saint Patrick

Part One.
About the three dwelling places: the kingdoms of God, Earth, and hell. The kingdom of God is good, and hell is bad.

There are three dwelling places under the power of God: the highest, the lowest, and the middle. Of them, the highest is called the kingdom of God or the kingdom of heaven, the lowest is named hell, and the middle is said to be the present world or the planet Earth. The two extremes are completely contrary to each other, and they have nothing in common. "For what partnership can light have with darkness, or how can Christ and the Devil agree?" (2 Corinthians 6:14, 15)

However, the middle has many similarities with both extremes. This is where light and darkness live, cold and warmth, sickness and health, rejoicing and grieving, hate and love, good and bad, just and unjust, masters and slaves, king and subject, famine and abundance, life and death, and countless others of this sort. In all of them, one side bears the likeness of heaven, and the other side has the image of hell. For in this world there is a mixture of bad people and good people. However, in heaven, there are no bad people, but all are good, and in hell, no one is good, but all are bad.

For both places are filled with people from this world; some are raised to heaven and others are dragged down to hell. Of course, the like are joined to the like, that is, the good with the good and the bad with the bad. Just men are joined to just angels, and transgressor men to transgressor angels. The servants of God are joined to God, and the servants of the devil are joined to the devil. The blessed are called to "the kingdom that has been prepared for them from the start of the world," and "the wicked are cast into the eternal fire, which has been prepared for the devil and his angels" (Matthew 25:34, 41).

However good the kingdom of heaven is said to be, no one clothed in flesh can know or understand what it is like, for the things there are much better and greater than what is thought of or understood. For this reason, Scripture says, "Eye has not seen, and ear has not heard, and no human mind has conceived what God has prepared for those who love him" (1 Corinthians 2:9). Therefore, the

45

kingdom of God is greater than all the reports, better than all praise, more immense than all knowledge, and more excellent than the glory that is believed. And likewise, no one can know or understand the evils of hell; surely, they are exceedingly worse than what is thought.

And so, the kingdom of God is full of light, and peace, and charity, and wisdom, and glory, and honesty, and sweetness, and love, and melodies, and joy, and eternal blessedness, and all the ineffable good that no one is able to say or think. And the place of hell is full of darkness, disorder, hate, foolishness, misery, foulness, bitterness, offenses, grief, burning, thirst, inextinguishable fire, sadness, eternal punishment, and all the ineffable bad that no one is able to say or to think. The citizens of heaven are the just men and angels; the all-powerful God is their king. And oppositely, the citizens of hell are wicked men and demons; the devil is their leader.

The sight of all the saints and angels satisfies the just, and the vision of God satisfies above all these. The sight of all the damned men and demons torments the impious and sinners, and the sight of the devil torments them above all these. In the kingdom of God, nothing that is desired goes unfound; and in hell, nothing that is found is desired. In the kingdom of God, nothing is found unless it pleases and delights and satisfies; on the other hand, in the pit, nothing is seen but eternal misery, and nothing is felt unless it displeases, offends, and causes pain.

In the eternal kingdom there will be life without death, truth without error, happiness without disturbance. All good, and no evil, abounds in the kingdom of God; all bad, and no good, abounds in the prison of the devil. No unworthy person is taken up into the kingdom of God; no truly worthy person, no just man, is dragged down to hell.

Part Two.
About the infernal punishments.

There are two principal torments in hell: unbearable cold and the heat of inextinguishable fire. For this reason, it is said in the Gospel, "In that place, there will be wailing and grinding of teeth" (Matthew 13:51, 22:13 and 25:50). For wailing and melting of the eyes comes from heat, and surely grinding of teeth comes from cold. Hence, also the blessed Job says, "They will pass from the waters of snows into extreme heat" (Job 24:19).

Numberless punishments are exacted through these two torments, as you can see: intolerable thirst, the punishment of hunger, the punishment of stench, the punishment of horror, the punishment of fear, the punishment of anguish, the punishment of darkness, the severity of the torturers, the presence of demons, the ferocity of beasts, the barbarity of the rulers, being torn apart by immortal vermin, the worms of conscience, the fire of tears, the sighs, the misery, the grief without a remedy, the unbroken chains, eternal death, punishment without end, the absence of Christ after the vision of him (which is called the greatest thing above all others), and all the other intolerable punishments.

Part Three.
About those whose love of the world is not deterred by the eternal punishments. The double punishment of hell. 100 years is no part of eternity.

Therefore, woe to those who deserve to enter under all these unceasing evils, without end, because of one sweet hour of sleep! For truly, all the glory of this world is but a dream, compared to eternal glory. It is better for those people to not have been born, as is said of unhappy Judas (Matthew 26:24), than to deserve to suffer the evil afflictions of hell.

What is more foolish, absurd and childish than being ensnared and overcome by the shadow and image and likeness of true glory, instead of seeking and desiring true delight, true beauty, true elegance, true honor? Who would prefer to neglect his own gold in favor of chasing after a twinkle of gold in water? Wouldn't that man be easily convinced by foolish and silly things? Or who, seeing a copy of the sun, would esteem the shape and materials of the copy more than the sun itself? Wouldn't that man be mocked by everyone? Thus, there is laughing, which is lower than crying, at whoever esteems the fragile things of this world, which are prone to fall.

This man prizes the useless love of flesh, he seeks it, and he strives after it, contemptuous of eternal glory and ignoring the ineffable joys of the kingdom of heaven. This is the business of exceedingly stupid men, of pitiable men, of men who do not possess healthy hearts, even if they have not sought the misfortunes of hell, which cannot be spoken of or imagined.

Truly, this is a double misfortune: to be apart from the kingdom of God and to always be in hell, that is, with the devil; to miss the presence of the angels and to always suffer the terrible presence of demons. No one can adequately describe how much this should be shunned, avoided and feared.

Who, being of sound mind, would choose 100 years of punishment for the delights of one day? But nevertheless, the pitiable men without any wisdom, following the love of flesh, do not avoid or escape intolerable punishments. These punishments do not last for 100 years, nor for 1,000 years, not even for 1,000 times 1,000 years, but for all ages without end, and yet people willingly accept these punishments for the sake of the delights of 40 or 60 years, or whatever perishable delight they choose.

How much difference is there between one day and 100 years? Obviously, it is less than the difference between eternity and 40 or 60 or 100 years, whether the future is in good places or in bad. For one day is just another part in the space of 100 years, an exceedingly tiny measure, and truly the space of 100 years is no part in that eternity. For, to speak freely, if 100 or 1,000 years were part of eternity, we could talk about the extent of eternity in terms of how many hundredfold or thousandfold years it is. It would then cease to be eternity, because reason does not set an end to eternity, which, if it could be limited by any time or measure, would not be eternity at all.

Part Four.
To depart from the broad way to the narrow path. The happiness of the blessed, their knowledge, the condition of their love. Of the ineffable sweetness of the vision of God.

Therefore, it is braver to resist fleshly desires, and it is better to fight against the deceitful enticements of this world and to be vigilant against the countless suggestions of Satan. For broad is the way of all those with a fondness for living, and this is "the way that leads to death" (Matthew 7:13). And truly, the desire of the whole heart is the narrow way that leads to life, which should be longed for and followed. This narrow way is the way of abstinence, chastity, humility, and all morality. Christ has set out this way before us; by this way he traveled to his kingdom. Let us also follow in his footsteps until we arrive after him in the royal city that he rules. Whatever man has said about this city is like a drop of the ocean, or like a spark in a fireplace. Anyone can see that the just "shine forth from this city like the sun" (Matthew 13:43), as the Lord said.

In that place, there will be the highest peace, the greatest ease, no work, no sadness, no poverty, and no old age, no death and no night at all, no desire for food and no burning thirst. But the food and drink of all will be the vision of Christ and the holy Trinity, and the contemplation of that Divinity by the pure eye of the heart, and, let me say it, the perpetual reading of the Book of Life, that is, of eternal truth and highest wisdom and the Word of God, which is the vision of Jesus Christ. Whereas now He is hidden from us, there He will be shown most clearly; there, many other things will be made clear: The reason why this man is chosen, and that man is a reprobate; why this man is assumed into the kingdom and that man is reduced to slavery; why one child died in the womb, another in infancy, another in youth and another in old age; why one man is poor and another is rich; why a child born out of adultery is baptized, and another child born from a legitimate marriage dies before baptism; why he who starts his life well would ever end his life badly, and why he who starts life badly often finishes well. All these things, and many other things like them, will be made plain and apparent in the Book of Life.

In that city, the reward of a single person becomes the reward of all, and the reward of all, through charity, will become the reward of one. There, every good thing will be open to all. There, all people will know one another's thoughts. There, no proud man will be superior, and no envious man will be inferior. For how can someone be envious of anyone when he esteems everyone else just as much as he esteems himself? Such a man would be jealous of no one.

In heaven, no one will desire to be better or superior than he already is, for it would be improper for the citizens of heaven to be in any way different from the way they already are. They are how they are because they deserved to become that way. Therefore, the person who is in heaven will not desire to be something other than what he is, but instead he will desire to be what he deserves to be; that is to say, he will be excellent, not only by himself alone, but also in the universal body of the heavenly Church. For in a body, if any part is set higher or lower than where it is by nature, the body becomes monstrous and hideous. Doubtless, in the same way, if anyone in the kingdom of God is placed higher than where morality and the will of the all-powerful creator demand he should be placed, it creates hideousness, not only on himself, but on the whole congregation.

Further, he who is the least in heaven, without a doubt, will have greater glory than he who owns the entire earth, even if he could live forever. For it is very cheap and worthless to take delight in simple things, to be delighted both by visible and physical things, in comparison to taking delight in and rejoicing in God himself. For such is the beauty of justice, such is the joy of eternal life (which is unchanging truth and wisdom), that even if we were not allowed to remain in heaven for more than one day, we would scorn a life on earth, a life full of delights and countless years, and we would scorn having continual bodily goods and favors. For not with false or with little love was it written: "One day within your courts is better than a thousand elsewhere" (Psalm 84:10).

Nothing is to be compared to the delight and rejoicing that is born from invisible and incorporeal things, and from the society of the angels and all the just, and from the sound knowledge and contemplation of that divine nature, and the face-to-face vision from God himself. God, whose beauty the angels admire; by whose power the dead are lifted up; whose "wisdom is not to be numbered" (Psalm 147:5); whose kingdom knows no end; whose glory cannot be told; whose light obscures the sun so much that, in comparison to him, the sun has no light; whose sweetness so transcends honey that, being compared with him, honey tastes like the bitterest wormwood. If all those imprisoned in the jail of hell saw God's face, they would feel no punishment, no grief, and no sadness. If his presence with the holy ones appeared in hell, it would immediately be converted into a pleasant paradise.

God, without whose approval not even a leaf falls from a tree; whose eyes penetrate the fiery depth of hell; whose ears hear the silent voice of the heart, that is, the thoughts of the heart; whose eyes hear as well as see, and whose ears see as well as hear, because they are not physical body parts, but they are the highest knowledge and certain thought. God, whose delights satisfy the hungry without any distaste. The blessed are found with God's delights, but they still always long for them; God's delights create hunger and thirst without pain, and they always satisfy the burning desire.

Seeing God's wonderful secrets, they are always new and

marvelous, creating amazement in their discerners, no more than when they start to be seen than after 1,000 years, or after 1,000 times 1,000 years. And with the angels who have been accustomed to see them even from the beginning of the world, they still admire them today no less than they did on the first day. Otherwise, the knowledge of the angels seeing God just now would seem cheap, compared to the hearts of the angels who have constantly been seeing God. God, whose knowledge of past and future things, is not in the past and in the future, but is in the present.

Part Five.

All things are present to God, without any prejudgment against human freedom. The discourse and praise of God. His existence before time. True evil is worse than false evil. The vision of God that is conferred upon the blessed. The eternity of God. The knowledge of God.

From this, we know that God does not see the day of judgment, and he does not see the first day of the ages, but he sees both. God's foreknowledge does not lead anyone towards sinning, as many mistaken people say. For if, they say, God knew ahead of time that Adam would become a sinner, it would have been impossible for Adam to avoid sinning. From this error is born the idea that God is the cause of sin, which is monstrous to say.

The people who say these things are tripped up by their own words. For if the things of which God has foreknowledge must occur, out of necessity, then man sinned by means of his own free will, and not out of any necessity, because in the foreknowledge of God man sinned by a free and voluntary decision, not led by necessity. Therefore, if the foreknowledge of God is unable to be avoided, humans are unable to sin through anything other than free will. They are led by no other power, because God foresees they will sin in this way. Therefore, if the decision to sin is voluntary, it is not forced. For if mankind is not forced to sin, then without a doubt, humans are able to avoid sin if they wish, and because humans willingly sin, they therefore deserve punishment. Otherwise, the punishment of death would not have been taken up by God.

God's discourse is hidden inspiration, which is how he invisibly shows his will and his love to minds. Perceiving this discourse, the angels obey God through everything. God's praise will be extolled by the chosen, and the manifestation by his chosen will show forth goodness to all people. Therefore, perpetual praise by the chosen will honor him—everlasting is his marvelousness. His wonderful measures do not come before the world and time, because there was no space of hours before the world, and in this way, God will always be without beginning.

For there was no time before time existed, but rather, time was co-created with the world. If time began to run at the same time as the world, then time was not made before the world. And therefore, as we said earlier, there was no time *before* time that God existed, and there was no time before the world that God existed, because time and his world are of the same age, for it was through God's motion that they both began to run. Whatever is moved exists before its own motion. And God existed before the world in infallible eternity, not in time. God's time was not before the world.

God's light dispels the darkness of ignorance, and it is through his light that we know that some portion of all these things which we say is true and certain. Through the same light, we see that truth is better than falsehood. And further, we see that evil discourse or true sin is worse than false evil or false sin, not on account of its truth, but on account of the fact that it is evil and sin. For something else cannot be evil or sin, unless it is true evil or sin; for false evil is not evil, just as false silver is not silver. Some people say that evil or sin comes from truth, and it is done in truth. In this way, they make evil out to be the work of truth, which is entirely false. For all that is true rises from the truth, and all that is true is also good, to the extent that it is true.

Consequently, a true thing comes from truth, so that if evil or sin exists, it does not exist in and of itself; in order to exist, that evil depends on another thing, a thing that is good and true. So, whatever is evil is not itself good, but nonetheless, it is true and good in that it exists. For evil does not exist by itself without the existence of good; in no way would God allow that to be done. Of course, the All-Powerful One makes many good things out of bad things, such as when he forms good from the adultery of men, and he makes them human again.

This and all other things we know about God are known through some portion of God's light, poured forth as if into a narrow crack in the ground. And if we know these things to be true, how much and what sort of knowledge and wisdom will be brought to light in heaven, where we will see that sun of truth face to face, that is, where we will know true and certain wisdom? God's presence makes the people who are near him become more like him. God's absence makes the people who are apart from him become less like him in every way. For true wisdom, true beauty and true eternity are close to God; therefore, the person who is also close to God will assuredly be wise and beautiful and eternal.

God's eternity is without beginning and without end (For if there was time when time didn't exist, who created it?), because he himself is the only God. Before him, there was no other god, there is no other god, and there will be none other. Not by chance did he create himself, and with nothing, he created himself, for by what power could he have made himself, when all powers besides himself were entirely nonexistent? Therefore, the only option left is to say that everything that is made is not God. Therefore, God was made without any means, without beginning, before all things were. For whatever is made has a beginning, and whatever has a beginning, without a doubt, is made, not made by someone other than God, but rather, God makes all things.

God's knowledge is without any variety of thought, and his mind does not wander here and there as he contemplates the innumerable truth of all creatures: angels, humans, stars (Hebrews 11:12), sands (Genesis 13:16), hair (Matthew 10:30), words (Psalm 139:4), thoughts, all moments. He perceives and understands them all at the same time and at once. Therefore, God is the fount and origin of knowledge; how much a person thirsts for this fountain will be how much he drinks from it (John 4:13-14).

Part Six.
The knowledge of the blessed. Of the threefold vision: physical, spiritual and intellectual.

Therefore, the society of the angels and the saints, and the presence of God himself, as we said earlier, incomparably surpasses the kingdom of the whole world, even if this world were to last forever.

In the vision of God, three types of knowledge are born: the human who discerns, and God who is discerned, and all the others who will see and understand everything. For it is just like the threefold vision that is brought to us through a glass mirror: we see ourselves, and the mirror itself, and whatever is present. Thus, through the mirror of divine clarity, we will see God himself—as much as this is possible for a creature—and we will see us ourselves, and we will know the other truths and certain knowledge.

At that time, by seeing God, we will see the hidden things of creation and hell itself. Then, it will be clear to the just how God is invisible, unequaled, without beginning and without end, before all things and after all things. They shall understand the Trinity, whatever is different about God being born, which pertains to the Son, and whatever is different about his procession, which pertains to the Holy Spirit, who is one from a single nature, while proceeding from two other persons. And it will be clear how the Father does not come before the Son or the Holy Spirit in time, but in origin; and how all things of God are one in God, receiving that which pertains to the relation of the Trinity.

For the wisdom and truth and eternity of God are not spread out, but are one in all respects. For the wisdom of God is not greater than the truth, and the truth is not greater than the wisdom, the eternity, or all the other things of God. For they are one in God, and not only these things are the same in God, but they are nothing other than God himself. And it will be revealed how goodness was in God, before it existed in itself, not good, but God; and how God is everywhere without location, how God is great without quantity, and how God is good without quality, and how God penetrates everything that is clean and unclean without becoming polluted. For if light that is visible can illumine all places and even penetrate manure without smell or without being polluted, then how much more God, who is invisible and unchangeable light, can enter all things without any change or pollution? God enters all things, rules all things, sustains all things, surrounds all things and illumines all things, not only the things of heaven and of earth, but of hell as well.

Then, there will be a threefold vision of God for the elect, that is: 1) a physical vision, which will be seen by bodies, some of which will have brilliancy like the sun, some like the moon, and others like the stars; 2) a spiritual vision, in the spirit, which resembles the physical vision and will not see false ideas (Further, the spirits of the just take delight in this vision today, from behind the barrier of the body); and 3) an intellectual vision, in the spirit, through which the pure eye of the mind sees God, and God's souls, and the most profound virtues, and angelic spirits.

Then, they will give double thanks to God, namely, thanks for their liberation from perpetual damnation and thanks for their reward of indescribable good. Then, all the public criminals and the devil's hosts will be damned in the sight of the elect of God; their damnation and intolerable punishment will stand out as a delectable spectacle to the elect. Then, with the most ardent love, they will love the giver of their liberation and of all good things. Without end and without pride, through the cry of the heart, they will praise God the all-powerful, the benign, and the merciful, to whom are the honor and the glory, both now and through all ages.

Amen.

The Book of Twelve Abuses of the Age

A Tract

Which Has Also Been Attributed to Saint Cyprian and Saint Augustine

Part 1.

The first abuse is the wise person without good works. They are like a preacher who teaches something in a sermon but fails to do it in their actions. The people who hear the teachings are told to defy them, when they notice the disconnect between the works of the preacher and the words of the preacher. For the authority of law will never be effective, unless it is attached to the listeners and carried out in works of the heart. If the wise preacher descends into a love of vice, it is like a doctor who pays little attention to the medicine of another doctor for their own wounds. For this reason, the Lord himself in the Gospel wished to instruct his disciples that teaching and good works are equally important. What a caution they had, when he admonished them, saying, "What if salt loses its flavor? In what can it be salted?" (Matthew 5:13). That is, if a wise person goes astray, who can set them on the right path again? "And if the light which is in you becomes darkness, how dark will it be!" (Matthew 6:23). For if an eye stops its job of seeing, what hand or foot or any other body part can perform that duty? Therefore, when wise people think they are not subjected to greater temptations, opportunities for sin appear much more abundantly. For even Solomon himself, while having much wisdom, committed a transgression. All the people of the kingdom of Israel were dispersed solely because of him. Therefore, the person to whom many things are committed loses more, if they have not correctly dispensed their duties which they possess. For more shall be taken away from the one to whom more is given: "The slave who knows his master's will and does not do it will be beaten with whips of punishment more heavily and more sharply" (Luke 12:47).

Part 2.

The second abuse is the old person found to be without religion. Their external human parts age, but their internal human parts, that is, the strength of the soul, do not gain increased power. For more than anything else, religion gives work to the senses. The senses bloom in the present age and retreat towards the end of life. Using wood as an example, the false tree is made visible, because after the enjoyment of the best flowers, they wither and do not show their own cultivation. It is the same way with humans, when the flower of youth has deserted the reprobate. In old age, the mature fruit of good works carries little weight. For what stupider thing can be done? If a mind does not attempt to hasten towards perfection while young, will they not be inclined to hasten towards death when old age comes upon their whole body? When the eyes darken, the ears hear heavily, the hair weakens, the face changes and becomes pale, the teeth fall out and diminish in number, the skin dries up, breath does not smell sweetly, the chest chokes, coughing is immoderate, knees tremble, ankles and feet swell; even a person who does not age interiorly is aggravated by all these things. And the fact that all these things will happen soon is already announced by the house of the body. For what remains, while death approaches in this life? There is nothing else to think about, other than how to prosper in the future, which every old person wants. To the young, the end of life stands uncertain, but older people know that the light of the senses will soon depart from them. Therefore, they are on guard against two things that do not grow old in the flesh and that drag the entire person into sin: namely, the heart and the tongue. The heart never stops putting new thoughts into motion, and the tongue quickly says whatever the heart feels. Therefore, beware the age of senility; do not let those two things ensnare you with their song, and stop foolishly ridiculing the heaviness of the body. For everyone should consider what age is worthy of greatness. No matter how you live, neither life, nor age, nor work returns cheaply.

Part 3.

The third abuse is the youth without obedience, because they are deprived of the purity that comes from rightly ordered reason. For if you refuse to show obedience to your elders when you are young, what kind of help will you expect to receive when you are old? This is why old people have a saying: "A person cannot be a ruler if they refused to serve others earlier." Because of this, Lord Jesus himself, when he was made flesh, obediently stood in service to his parents. He did not approach the teachers in the temple until he was the lawful age. Therefore, just as sobriety in the senses and perfection of the will are required, so also obedience; yielding and submissiveness are rightfully owed in adolescence. This is also why, in the Ten Commandments, the first law pertaining to humans demands that you honor your father and mother, because they will not outlive you, or it will never be unworthy. To a father who is worthy and living, paternal honor should be offered by the children up to the dignity of the age. Truly, people are called "father" in four ways through divine Scripture: by nature, race, reminder and age. About a natural father, Jacob says to Laban, "If the fear of my father Isaac had not been with me, you would have taken everything that is mine" (Genesis 31:42). And about a father by race, when the Lord spoke to Moses from the bush, it is said, "I am the God of your fathers, the God of Abraham, the God of Isaac, the God of Jacob" (Exodus 3:6). And a father by age and reminder are both discussed when Moses says in the song of Deuteronomy, "Ask your father, and it will be shown to you. Ask your elders, and they will tell you" (Deuteronomy 32:7). Therefore, it does not matter if you survive your natural parents, or if they are unworthy. So listen if you want the obedience of youth to be shown to you when you are old. How is it possible for someone to be honored in old age if they did not endure the work of discipline in adolescence? Truly, a person reaps whatever they have sowed. "For at the time, all discipline is not seen as a cause for joy, but for sorrow. Later, it gives back the most peaceful fruit of holiness" (Hebrews 12:11). Just as fruit is not found in a tree that did not have leaves or flowers earlier, so also someone cannot receive lawful honor in old age who did not do any work in youthful discipline. And if discipline happens without obedience, what kind of discipline can it be? Therefore, a youth without discipline is a youth without obedience, because obedience itself, which is the mother of all discipline, requires much work. You should take the Lord Christ's example of exertion as your own; he "was obedient to the father, even to death" (Philippians 2:8). He willingly endured the disgrace of the cross.

Part 4.

The fourth abuse is the rich person without charity, who is generous when it comes to guarding and protecting his own money, but who does not distribute anything to the needy and those who have nothing. While the rich seek to guard their fortunes with great care, they lose the everlasting treasure of the heavenly father. About this treasure, when the rich young man asked the Lord Jesus about perfection, Jesus challenged him, responding, "If you wish to be perfect, go and sell all that you have, and give it to the poor, and come, follow me, and you will have treasure in heaven" (Matthew 19:21). No person can ever have this treasure, unless they are a consolation to the poor, or they are poor themselves. Therefore, do not sleep in your treasure while paupers are not able to sleep. For even if you collect many riches, you will not at all be able to delight in them alone, because the nature of one person does not help many things. Therefore, what is more foolish than a person who, because of food and clothing, loses the whole kingdom of heaven and everlasting happiness, and instead they enter the eternal torment of hell without consolation? So according to God's will, whatever is lost through necessity is exchanged for eternal reward. "For all which are seen are temporary, but those things which are not seen are eternal" (2 Corinthians 5:18). For while we are temporary, we are subject to temporary things, and when we pass from here, we take on eternal comforts forever. So we should not prize the things that we will not always have; especially when the greedy show off their own riches, treasure, lands, and all that they have, without reason. A single look shows that the greedy love those things with their whole hearts, even though they are things that you should never esteem. For if they love gold and silver and lands and clothes and drinks and metals and brute animals, none of these things can return that love. Nature shows this. For what is more ridiculous than to love something that cannot love you? And to neglect that which offers all love for your love? For this reason, we should not love the world, but love to closely follow the commands of God, because the person who is close to God has their love returned, which the world cannot do in the least. For the Lord commands us to love our enemies; that love makes a friend out of an enemy. Whoever wants to be rich, to have eternal wealth, they will not endure without distributing to the needy. For if they do not sell what they love, no one can buy what they desire. The greed is called a curse from the most high justice, because the ones who pass by their houses do not say, "The blessing of the Lord upon you, we bless you in the name of the Lord" (Psalm 128:8). Therefore, the ones who love money are unhappy because they love temporary things, and they will perish in eternal damnation. On the other hand, "Blessed are the merciful, for they will be shown mercy" (Matthew 5:7). Therefore, the merciful person is happy, because in this virtue, God requires good will, not worldly possessions.

Part 5.

The fifth abuse is the woman without modesty. For just as all good practices care for and guard prudence in men, all acts of honor cultivate, encourage and guard modesty in women. For modesty guards chastity, restrains greed, avoids fights, alleviates anger, masters lust, tempers passion, corrects lewdness, guards against drunkenness, does not multiply words, purges the appetite for sin and entirely condemns secrecy. What else? It restrains all vices. It nourishes all virtues and whatever is praiseworthy to the heart of God and good humans. For an immodest life neither receives praise from people in the present age, nor does it expect a reward from God in the future. Truly, a modest life has a good reputation among people and rejoices in the hope of future happiness. In the present, modesty makes itself imitable; afterwards, it leaves behind a lovely memory. It always attracts and agrees with good practices and arouses the soul with eloquent and constant thoughts of Scripture. It guards the examples of good ancestors and joins with the intimate company of perfection. Therefore, the exercise of true modesty comes in two ways: the disposition of the body and the soul's concern for things above and below. Through the exterior mode, before God, we prepare good works. For modesty is of the body, not to desire strange things, and to avoid all uncleanness, to not want to eat before the correct time, to not rouse laughter, to not speak false and vain words. It is a bringing together of all order, and being properly composed, even if you are wearing hair clothes. It does not go into unworthy dwellings; it looks at no one with a haughty gaze; it does not allow the eyes to wander, it does not move with showy and cruel steps, it sees nothing inferior in starting good work, it produces no insults or shame, it blasphemes no one, it does not laugh at old age, it does not envy good things, it does not fight with better people. Do not discuss things that you don't know, and do not reveal everything about that which you do know, for these things give love to neighbors and make you acceptable to God. Modesty is of the soul, because it does all good works in the eyes of God, rather than in the eyes of humans. It restrains the appetite for wicked thoughts. It envies no one but seeks to make itself better in all things. The modest do not rely upon themselves, but they always commit to God as a helper in all things. Modesty stations itself before the eyes of God. It does not stain the senses with heretical depravity, but it agrees with Catholicism through all things. It clings to God alone. It offers chastity of the eternal mind to Christ God. It knows that death is the beginning of all good things. With bravery of the soul, it disregards and thinks little of present trials. Therefore, it loves nothing on earth except neighbors, it stations a treasure of all love in heaven and, through all good deeds, looks for a reward from God in the heavens. Modesty is a celebrated decoration, the elevation of humility, the excellence of the unknown, the beauty of the weak, the success of labors, the solace of the seas, the growth of all beauty, the glory of religion, the defense of crime, the multiplication of benefits, the friendship of God, the creator of all.

Part 6.

The sixth abuse is the ruler without virtue, because it is useless to have the power of ruling if the ruler does not have rigor of virtue. But this rigor of virtue is not so much exterior bravery—which is also necessary for ruling in the world—as it is bravery of the interior soul. It must be exercised. For often the bravery of rulers is lost by neglecting the soul, just like what happened to the priest Eli. He could not restrain his sinner sons with the severity of a judge. When punishing them, the Lord was fiercely unsparing, as is fitting. Therefore, three things are necessary for those who are ruled: namely, terror, order and love. For unless the ruler is equally loved and feared, his order can hardly last long. So the rulers ensure they are loved, through favors and kindness, and they wish to be feared, through just punishments, not of their injuries, but the law of God. Also for that reason, since many people depend on the ruler, the rules should cling to God, who stationed them in leadership, who strengthened them mightily, for bearing the burdens of many.

For unless a peg is powerfully strengthened well and clings to something more powerful, the tent and everything that depends on it will quickly collapse. And so a ruler, released from the rigor of their own strength, will collapse to the ground under their burdens. So also, a prince and all that he holds together will quickly perish if he has not adhered perseveringly to his Maker. For some people approach God more through the job of ruling; some people worsen the honor of dignity when they are established as rulers. For Moses, accepted as ruler by the people, enjoyed being more familiar to God with his speech. Truly, Saul, the child of Sis, after he took the scepter of king, offended God through the arrogance of disobedience. King Solomon obtained the throne after his own father, David. God enriched him with the gift of wisdom above all other mortals, along with governorship over numberless people. And the opposite is true of Jeroboam, the servant of Solomon, after he seized part of the house of David. He diverted 10 tribes of Israel to the cult of idols which were in that part of Samaria. Through these examples it is clearly shown that some increase to greater perfection in a higher state, while others pass away to a worse state through the pride of ruling. We know through these examples that those who rise and become better are able to do so through virtue of the soul and the help of God, and those who take a turn for the worse fail equally through weakness of the mind and negligence. From this, we see there should not be a ruler without virtue. In no way do they have virtue without God as a helper. For a protector of many people cannot lead without bravery of the soul, since the greatest people are accustomed to work against great disturbances or adversity. For they should first look after the people they rule, with all effort of the soul, so that through all, no one can at all doubt that God is their helper. For if the ruler has the Lord of lords as a helper in their actions, no person will be able to be ruled by them with scorn: "For there is no power except the power that comes from God" (Romans 13). For God raises up the poor from the dung and makes them sit with the rulers of his people, and "He pulls down princes from their thrones and exalts the lowly" (Luke 1:52). May the whole world be placed under God, and let the glory of God be desired.

Part 7.

The seventh abuse is the contentious Christian, who took up a sharing of the name of Christ through faith and Baptism, but against the words and way of Christ, they love the amusements of the fallen world. For they love everything they fight about, whether through love of the thing itself, or another love that hides under hateful appearance. To explain, someone may fight a war against a hateful thing with spirited strikes because they love victory and freedom. And many other kinds of love are desired with contention, under hateful work or fear. From this, it is clearly known, nothing can be desired unless it is desired through love, hope, and a lovely repayment afterwards. So whoever has reason to fight over the present world makes it clear that they love the world. The words of the Holy Spirit say how much the world should be loved, through John, who says, "Do not love the world, nor the things that are in the world" (1 John 2:15). For love of the world and God cannot coexist equally in one heart, just as the same eyes never equally see heaven and earth. But if there is truly something or someone in the world who should be loved, it must be remembered that the divine utterance forbids them to be loved. Therefore, it is commanded not to love the earth, with those born in it, and its metals, and living beings, and the beauty of clothing, and delights of food, and those things that are related to these. But rather, it is commanded to love neighbors, for whom all these things were made. For all these I mentioned do not remain permanently; they cannot be brought with you when you go to the heavenly homeland. Now, neighbors who are co-heirs of the king remain permanently and love each other freely. For it is ordered not to love the world, and what does not always remain in the world, and will disappear along with the world. But neighbors are part of the heavenly kingdom, on earth and among the last elements, so it is not inconsistent for those striving for the heavenly kingdom to love their neighbors, when they will be co-heirs in that highest homeland for eternity. Therefore, truly, it is commanded not to love the present world, nor anything strange from love of God, which makes you a lover of the present age. So no one should be contentious about what is not allowed to be loved. Therefore, a Christian, who has a resemblance to the name of Christ should also have a resemblance to the behavior of Christ. For no one is rightly called "Christian" unless they are equal to Christ in behavior. Truly, it is written about Christ through the Prophet, "Behold my son whom I chose, my chosen one. My soul is greatly pleased in him. I will place my spirit upon him. He will not be contentious or complain, and no one will hear his voice in the street." (Isaiah 42:1-2; Matthew 12:18) Behold, Christ was not contentious, nor did he complain. And you, if you wish to have a resemblance to the behavior of Christ, you must not be contentious nor appear abusive in the Christian Church. For Christ has commanded his followers, "Do not be called 'rabbi,' for you have one Father, who is in heaven. So all of you are brothers." (Matthew 23:8). Christ commands about praying to the Father when he says, "Therefore, you will pray in this way: Our Father, who is in heaven, your name be holy." Therefore, a person claims to have a father on earth in error, when their prayer confesses they have their father and fatherland in heaven. No one is made a possessor of that fatherland unless they are free from contention of the earthly fatherland.

Part 8.

The eighth abuse is the proud pauper, who, having nothing, is elevated in pride, when it is commanded through the apostle Paul to not be proud of the opposite of the riches of the world. For what can be more foolish than someone who, through weak misery like the fallen earth, should be saddened and walk humbly and lowly, but instead, they lift up a mind inflated with a supercilious tumor of pride against God? When constructing the highest heavens, those people were a roof that has plunged down like a fallen vine, through pride. For who wishes to be proud on earth, like a powerful person, who should appear humble before all people? But those who do not have sadness about their own poverty should pay attention to what the poor receive from God. For he says, "Blessed are the poor in spirit, because the kingdom of heaven is theirs" (Matthew 5:3). For with good management, the merciful judge of the kingdom of heaven oversees those who had a sharing of the earthly kingdom among mortals. In heaven, riches appear by the seat of those who had nothing on earth. Therefore, paupers, while they pass through the earthly kingdom by want and necessity, should take care that they are not dismissed from the heavenly kingdom through a shameless mind. For when they received necessary poverty by the judgment of God, their judgment depends on whether they are poor in spirit. For the kingdom of heaven is not promised to whoever is poor, but to those whose lack of riches is accompanied by humility of the soul. For a humble pauper is called "poor in spirit" if they are never elevated in pride when they are seen as needy in public. Since humility strengthens the mind towards desiring the kingdom of heaven more, what riches poverty has in the present age! For the humble who rightly have these wealthy possessions can be called poor in spirit. But the proud ones who have nothing are certainly deprived of the beatitude of poverty. About such people it is said in Holy Scripture, "It is a person who has nothing, pretending to be rich, and it is a person with many riches, pretending to be poor" (Proverbs 13:7). Therefore, the wealth of the poor in spirit is pretending to be poor when you have many riches; and those who pretend to be rich, while having nothing, are the poor afflicted with a proud mind. Therefore, it is well-known that the humble mind is in need, while a swollen soul is filled with foolish riches. Therefore, the poor should take care that they know what they are like. And because they are not able to follow what they love, they should end the swollen pride of the mind.

Part 9.

The ninth abuse is the unjust king. A king should not be unjust, but rather, a king should correct injustice. For this reason, they themselves should guard the dignity of their own name. For it is understood that the name of "king" means this: that they attend to the office of ruler for all their subjects. But how can someone correct others when his own behavior is unjust and uncorrected? Since the throne of a king is exalted in justice, the king's guidance over the people is also strengthened in truth. Truly, the justice of a king is to unjustly oppress no one through power, to judge justly among men and their neighbors without regard of persons, to be the defense of strangers and orphans and widows, to stop robberies, to punish adulteries, to not exalt the unjust, to not nourish shamelessness and boasters, to banish the wicked from the land, to not allow father-killers and perjurers to live, to defend churches, to support the poor with alms, to station legitimate business above the king, to have old and wise and sober advisers, to not maintain superstitions of magic, fortune telling and witches, to delay anger, to defend the homeland bravely and justly against adversaries, to trust in God through all things, to not raise the soul to prosperity, to endure patiently in adverse circumstances, to have Catholic faith in God, to not allow their children to lead wicked lives, to insist on prayers at certain hours, and not to eat food before the proper time. "For woe to the land whose king is a child, and whose princes eat very early in the morning!" (Ecclesiastes 10:16). Just kings make prosperity in the present, and they lead the kingdom to the better, heavenly kingdom. Whoever manages a kingdom that does not follow this law will surely endure many hostilities of power. For that reason, the peace of the people is often broken, and they raise up stumbling blocks for the kingdom, and the fruit of the land is dashed to pieces, and the people are shackled in slavery, they infect the prosperity of the kingdom with many and various sorrows, they unite sadness with the deaths of free and happy citizens, they destroy enemies everywhere in the province, they tear apart the cattle, beasts and flocks of farmers. They ruin work, like storms of winter, the air and the sea destroy the fertility of the land. They burn up cornfields and the flowers of trees and the vine like strikes of lightning. Above all, the injustice of the king not only darkens the form of power in the present, but also clouds their children and relatives should they hold inheritance to the kingdom afterwards. For because of the guilt of Solomon, the Lord dispersed the kingdom of the house of Israel from the hands of Solomon's sons. And because of the justice of king David, the Lord allowed the lamp of his offspring to always remain in Jerusalem (1 Kings 11:31-35). Behold how much the justice of the king flourishes in the age; it is clearly obvious to those who look. For it is the peace of the people, the defense of the homeland, the freedom of the commoners, the protection of the race, the cure of weariness, the joy of humans, the temperature of the air, the calmness of the sea, the fertility of the land, the solace of the poor, the inheritance of children and to themselves, they are the hope of future happiness. Nevertheless, the king should know that just as he was placed first among men on the throne, so also he will bear primacy in punishment if he did not make justice. For regarding all the sinners that the king has under himself in the present, no matter who they are, the king will have their future punishment placed above him in an unpleasant way.

Part 10.

The tenth abuse is the negligent bishop. His station requires honor among people, but he does not guard the worthiness of his office in the presence of God, even though he serves as God's ambassador. For first of all, if someone would have the dignity of the name "bishop," he must understand that he is a sentinel. Truly, why he is made a sentinel, and what is required from a sentinel, the Lord himself reveals. When under the person of Ezekiel the prophet, he declares his reasoning to the Bishop, saying this: "I have given you as a sentinel to the house of Israel. Therefore, when you hear a speech from my mouth, you will announce it to them, from me. So if you see a sword coming, and you do not announce to the people to turn from their wicked ways, then the wicked will die in their sin, but I will consider their blood to be on your hands. But if you announce to them, and they do not turn from their ways, then the wicked will die in their sin, but you will have saved your soul" (Ezekiel 3:17-19). Thus, a bishop, who is placed as the sentinel of all should attentively give heed to sins, and after he has considered, he should amend for sins with words and deeds, if he can. If he cannot, he should shun the workers of evil, following the example of the Gospel. "For if," the Lord says in the Gospel, "your brother has sinned against you, reproach him, between you and him alone. If he should listen to you, you will have saved your brother. If he should not listen to you, bring one or two witnesses with you, so that every word is established on the testimony of two or three witnesses. If your brother should not listen to them, treat him like a foreigner or a tax collector." (Matthew 18:15). Whoever is not willing to cling to this command should be rejected as teacher or bishop. And someone who is rejected by this command should not be received by another teacher or bishop. For about priests, it is written in the law: "Do not marry a divorced or widowed woman" (Leviticus 21:7). Therefore, if a priest gets married to someone unpermitted, he oversteps the laws of the holy priesthood. He should be excommunicated from the Catholic Church by the bishop, for the sake of those he serves as an overseer. As for the other qualifications, Paul the Apostle explains: "… coming to the rank of Bishop, he should be sober, prudent, chaste, wise, modest, hospitable, having children under control with every purity, having good testimony from those who are outsiders, producing faithful homilies of teaching. Before he is a Bishop, he should not have more than one wife. He should not be a murderer, not deceitful, not a drunk, not a neophyte, because through these deeds, he shows that he believes something other than what he preaches and teaches." (1 Timothy 3:2-8). Therefore, let negligent bishops beware that the Lord will lament them in the time of his coming, saying through the Prophet, "Silent shepherds have destroyed my people, and my shepherds did not feed the flock, but fed themselves" (Ezekiel 34:8). But those who procure more, God places them in charge of the household, to give out food and measures of wheat in their own time. As you know, the food they give is pure and proven teachings, so that, when the Lord comes, they deserve to hear, "Well done, good and faithful servant, because you were faithful in small matters, I will place you above many people. Enter into the joy of your lord." (Matthew 25:23)

Part 11.

The eleventh abuse is the community without order, which, when it does not perform exercises of discipline, chains the community with snare of hell. For you cannot evade the anger of the Lord without the rigor of discipline. The cries of the Psalmist warn about these undisciplined people: "Learn discipline, lest the Lord become angry" (Psalm 2:12). Truly, the habit of discipline is improving yourself and observing the examples of the great ones who came before. About this discipline, Paul the Apostle says this: "Persevere in discipline. Offer yourselves to God, like children. But if you are without discipline, whose inheritance do you share in? For you are all bastards, and not children" (Hebrews 12:8). Therefore, those without discipline are bastards, and they do not take inheritance of the heavenly kingdom. But if they bear the corrections of paternal discipline, they are children, and they cannot despair of receiving an inheritance someday. And about this discipline, Isaiah warns of the undisciplined community, saying, "Stop your perverse ways. Learn to do good." (Isaiah 1:16). And to them, the Psalmist sings with a harmonious voice, saying, "Turn away from evil, and do good" (Psalm 23:15). Therefore, unhappy are they who reject discipline. For those who reject the discipline of Christ's church dare more than the soldiers who, when the Lord was crucified, did not dare to rip his tunic. For just as the tunic covers the whole body except the head, so discipline protects and adorns the whole church, except Christ, who is the head of the Church and is not under discipline. Truly, that tunic had woven over all from above, because that discipline of the Church is bestowed and restored by the Lord of heaven. When the Lord ascended to the Father, after he resurrected from the dead, he spoke about this to his Apostles, saying, "So you stay here in the city, until you are covered with virtue from on high" (Luke 24:49). Therefore, the tunic of the body of Christ is the discipline of the Church. Whoever is without discipline is foreign to the body of Christ. "So let us not tear it but let us cast lots to see whose it will be" (John 19:24). That is, let us not loosen any of the commands of the Lord, but whatever a person is called to, let him stay in it before the Lord.

Part 12.

The twelfth abuse is people without law, who, while they disregard the words of God and ordinances of the law, rush to the trap of hell through various ways of error. About these ways, under the character of a sinning people, the Prophet thus deplores the human race: "So we have wandered like sheep, each one of us turns away onto their own path." (Isaiah 53:6). And about these ways, Wisdom says through Solomon, "People see many paths as straight, but in the end, most of them lead to death" (Proverbs 14:12). Surely, then, many people follow these ways of ruin, when, through negligence, they abandon the one regal pathway—namely, the law of God—which does not turn aside to the left or the right. About this way, the Lord Jesus Christ, who is the end of law to justice for all believers, declares, "I am the way, the truth and the life, and no one comes to the Father except through me" (John 14:6). He invites all humans universally to the way, saying, "Come to me, all who labor and are burdened, and I will renew you" (Matthew 11:28); "Because it is not an acceptance of persons before God" (Romans 2:11), where "There is not Jew, nor Greek, male and female, servant and free, Roman and Scythian, but Christ is all in all: For all are one in Christ Jesus." (Galatians 3:28). When Christ is the end of law, whoever is without law is without Christ. Therefore, the people without law is a people without Christ. So it is an abuse for a people to be without law in times of the Gospel when unbounded license is given to the Apostles' preaching to all peoples; when the thunder of the Gospel has thundered through all parts of the age; when nations that previously did not follow justice have now learned justice; when those who lived a long way off have been made near in the blood Christ—they once were not a people, but now are the people of God in Christ; when it is the acceptable time, and the day of deliverance and the time of consolation in the sight of the Most High; when a single people has the witness of resurrection, the time the Lord himself bore witness to, saying, "Behold, I am with you for all days, up to the ending of the age" (Matthew 28:20). Let us not be without Christ in this transitory time, lest Christ be without us in the future.

Part 3

Miscellaneous Texts

Alphabetical Hymn

Written in praise of Saint Patrick, while he was alive.
Attributed to Saint Secundinus.

All who love God, hear the holy deeds
   Of Patrick the Bishop, the blessed man in Christ
   How the good from his work was like the angels
   And perfect, because his life was equal to the apostles.

Blessed of Christ, he kept God's commands in all things,
   Whose works shine like a light among humans,
   Who follow his holy, wonderful example
   Here and in heaven, glorifying God the Father.

Constant in love of God and with unchanging faith,
   He built up the Church like Peter,
   And whose apostleship is chosen by God
   Against whom the gates of hell do not prevail.

Designated by the Lord to teach the barbarian
   Nations, to fish with nets of doctrine,
   To bring the believers of the age to grace,
   And to follow the Lord to the eternal throne.

Elected by Christ, he sold Gospel talents,
   Which still collect interest among the Irish Gentiles.
   He worked diligently. The reward for the work
   Is to possess the joy of the heaven kingdom with Christ

Faithful minister of God, messenger of honor,
   He gave the model and example of Apostles.
   With words and deeds, he preached to the people,
   So whoever was not converted by words was called by good
deeds.

Glory he has with Christ, honor in the world.
   He is honored by all, like an Angel of God
   Whom God sent as an Apostle, like Paul to the Gentiles,
   To bring guidance to all, to the kingdom of God.

Humble in spirit and body, because of his fear of God,
  The Lord rests above him, because of his good work.
  He bears the wounds of Christ in his flesh.
  He glories in Christ's cross as his only support.

Indefatigable, he feeds the believers with the heavenly feast,
  So those who are seen with Christ do not fall off the way.
  He pays out Gospel words to them like bread,
  Which is multiplied in their hands, like manna.

Chaste[1], he guarded his flesh out of love of God.
  He prepared his flesh like a temple of the Holy Spirit.
  He is constantly possessed with clean actions
  So he offers his life to the Lord as a pleasing sacrifice.

Light of the world, greatly inflamed by the Gospel,
  Raised in a candelabra, he lit up the entire age,
  Citizen of the King, placed safe upon the mountain,
  Rich in many things that God possesses.

"Mightiest" he will be called in the kingdom of heaven,
  He who taught with sacred words, full of good works.
  He leads the way as a good example and faithful kind,
  And he has trust in God with a clean heart.

The Name of Lord he boldly preaches to the people,
  to whom he gives the grace of eternal clean health.
  He prays to God for their trespasses.
  For them, he offers up worthy sacrifices to God.

Opposing the glory of the world, he scorns it for divine law.
  To his mind, he esteems it all as rubbish.
  And he is not moved by the violent flood of this world
  But he rejoices in adversity, when he suffers for Christ.

---

[1] Latin does not have the letter "J." "K" is a placeholder for the Greek letter
kappa (K), which is usually replaced with the letter "C."

Pastor good and faithful, shepherd of Gospel
  Who was chosen to guard the nation of God
  And to feed his people with divine teachings,
  He has given up his soul for them, following the example of
Christ.

Questing ceaselessly, the Savior raised him to a Bishop
  So he could teach priests in heavenly warfare.
  He dispenses heavenly food and clothes to them,
  Which are discharged with divine and holy sermons.

Royal announcer, inviting believers to the marriage,
  Who is dressed and decorated with a wedding garment,
  Who draws heavenly wine in heavenly vessels
  And gives the spiritual chalice to the people of God.

Sacred treasure he finds in the holy book,
  And he provides the Divinity of the Savior in the flesh
  Who bought treasure with his holy and perfect service.
  He is called "Israel." His soul sees God.

Testifying for the Lord, faithful in Catholic law,
  His words are seasoned by the divine oracle.
  They do not rot and get eaten by worms, like human flesh,
  But they are salted with heavenly flavor for the victim.

Valued and true worker of the field of the Gospel
  Whose seeds are in the Gospel of Christ
  Whose plants divine with his mouth, in prudent ears,
  The Holy Spirit tills their hearts and minds.

X^2 (Christ) chose him to be his vicar on earth,
  Who frees slaves from a double captivity.
  He releases many from human slavery.
  He sets countless free from the rule of the devil.

Hymns[3] with Revelation and psalms of God, he sings,

---

[2] "X" is used in place of "Christ," in the same way "Xmas" can be used in place of "Christmas."

[3] The author wrote "hymn" without an "H" at the start of the word, presumably

Which draw the people towards building God.
He believes the law, in the name of the holy Trinity
He teaches that God is One in Three Persons and substance.

Zion, clothed with the Lord, day and night,
  Without ceasing the Lord prays to God,
  Who will receive the reward of his great labor
  When he rules with the holy Apostles over Israel.

In the Colgan version, this is added to the transcript.

Listen:

I always say the praises of Patrick, so God defends us with him.
All the Irish cry to you, like children:
"Come, holy Patrick, make us saved!"
May Saint Patrick the Bishop pray for us all
That our sins which we committed may be erased immediately.
Amen.

---

because they couldn't think of another word that starts with "Y." In Latin, "Y" is a placeholder for the Greek letter upsilon (Y).

The Breastplate of Saint Patrick
(The original is written in Irish, not Latin.)

I arise today
Through a mighty strength, the invocation of the Trinity,
Through a belief in the Threeness,
Through confession of the Oneness
Of the Creator of creation.

I arise today
Through the strength of Christ's birth and his baptism,
Through the strength of his Crucifixion and his burial,
Through the strength of his Resurrection and his Ascension,
Through the strength of his descent for the judgment of doom.

I arise today
Through the strength of the love of cherubim,
In obedience of angels,
In service of archangels,
In the hope of resurrection to meet with reward,
In the prayers of patriarchs,
In preachings of the apostles,
In faiths of confessors,
In innocence of virgins,
In deeds of righteous men.

I arise today
Through the strength of heaven;
Light of the sun,
Splendor of fire,
Speed of lightning,
Swiftness of the wind,
Depth of the sea,
Stability of the earth,
Firmness of the rock.

I arise today
Through God's strength to pilot me;
God's might to uphold me,
God's wisdom to guide me,
God's eye to look before me,
God's ear to hear me,
God's word to speak for me,
God's hand to guard me,
God's way to lie before me,
God's shield to protect me,
God's hosts to save me
From snares of the devil,
From temptations of vices,
From everyone who desires me ill,
Afar and anear,
Alone or in a multitude.

I summon today all these powers between me and evil,
Against every cruel merciless power that opposes my body and soul,
Against incantations of false prophets,
Against black laws of pagandom,
Against false laws of heretics,
Against craft of idolatry,
Against spells of women and smiths and wizards,
Against every knowledge that corrupts man's body and soul.
Christ shield me today
Against poison, against burning,
Against drowning, against wounding,
So that reward may come to me in abundance.

Christ with me, Christ before me, Christ behind me,
Christ in me, Christ beneath me, Christ above me,
Christ on my right, Christ on my left,
Christ when I lie down, Christ when I sit down,
Christ in the heart of every man who thinks of me,
Christ in the mouth of every man who speaks of me,
Christ in the eye that sees me,
Christ in the ear that hears me.

I arise today
Through a mighty strength, the invocation of the Trinity,
Through a belief in the Threeness,
Through a confession of the Oneness
Of the Creator of creation.

Made in the USA
Monee, IL
01 February 2023

26084611R00049